CHALLENGE
Mark Link, S.J.

**A meditation program
based on
*The Spiritual Exercises of St. Ignatius***

TABOR
PUBLISHING

Valencia, California   Allen, Texas

Imprimi Potest
Robert A. Wild, S.J.

Unless otherwise noted, Scripture passages are taken from
The New American Bible with Revised New Testament
© 1970, 1986 by the Confraternity of Christian Doctrine,
Washington, D.C. All rights reserved.

Photo Credits

Front cover: Darrell Ray Jones/The Stock Market
Black-and-white photography: Mark Link, S.J.

Send all inquiries to:
Tabor Publishing
25115 Avenue Stanford, Suite 130
Valencia, California 91355

Printed in the United States of America

ISBN 0-89505-654-2 (*Challenge*)
ISBN 0-89505-655-0 (*Decision*)
ISBN 0-89505-656-9 (*Journey*)

2 3 4 5   91 90 89 88

CONTENTS

Author's Preface

Physical exercises—swimming, climbing, hiking—are ways to improve circulation, breathing, and muscle tone. In short, they are ways to improve physical fitness and bodily health.

"Spiritual exercises"—meditation, contemplation, vocal prayer—are ways to do the same for the human spirit. In short, they are ways to improve spiritual fitness and spiritual health. The "spiritual exercises," or meditations, in *Challenge* have to do with spiritual fitness and spiritual health.

Challenge is the first phase of a three-phase meditation program called The Challenge Program. The second phase is presented in a companion book called *Decision;* the third phase, in a final book called *Journey.*

The Challenge Program, which is based on *The Spiritual Exercises of St. Ignatius,* was piloted in two different settings:

1. with adults of Saint Elizabeth Seton parish in Plano, Texas, and

2. with students at Jesuit High School in Dallas.

Brief descriptions of how The Challenge Program was implemented in these settings are found in Appendix A of this book.

The author is especially grateful to Father Patrick Koch and Father Patrick Phillips of Jesuit High, and to Maggie Herrod of the DRE staff of Saint Elizabeth Seton for their invaluable assistance.

January 1988   Mark Link, S.J.

HOW TO USE THIS BOOK

Master	*As the fish dies on the land, so you die in the midst of worldly business. To live again, the fish returns to water. You must return to solitude.*
Disciple	*Must I therefore leave my business and go into a monastery?*
Master	*Certainly not. Hold on to your business and go back to your heart.*

Anthony de Mello, S.J.

Challenge is designed to help you hold on to your business and go back to your heart. The meditation exercises in *Challenge* are based on *The Spiritual Exercises of St. Ignatius.* Normally, these exercises are made in a retreat house, where retreatants devote themselves to them full time for thirty days.

Saint Ignatius realized, however, that many people could not take thirty days off to do this. So, in the 19th Annotation of his Exercises, he explains how the meditations can be made at home over a longer period of time. *Challenge* is designed to help you do just that.

An ideal way to use *Challenge* is under the direction of a spiritual guide and as part of a support group that meets weekly. The role of the spiritual guide is discussed in Appendix B. The group meetings are discussed in Appendix C.

A second way to use *Challenge* is alone, under the direction of a spiritual guide.

A final way is by yourself, without a guide or a support group. This is not the best way, but it may be the only way possible for you. If you follow this option, try to consult occasionally with a spiritual guide.

This brings us to the "spiritual exercises," or meditations, in *Challenge*.

Someone said, "Most books are to be tasted. Some are to be tasted and savored. But only a few are to be tasted, savored, and digested." *Challenge* is the latter type of book. Its meditations are to be tasted, savored, and digested. In other words, they are to be—

- explored with your mind,
- pondered with your heart,
- sounded in your soul—that is, you listen with the ear of your soul to what God may wish to say to you through the meditations.

Before proceeding to the meditations in this book, let's answer a few questions about meditation in general.

Where should you meditate?

*"Go to your . . . room, close the door,
and pray to your Father."*   Matthew 6:6

Some people can meditate while riding a bus, walking to work, or sitting on a park bench. But if you want to meditate without interruption, you need to find a private place.

A private place has obvious advantages. For example, you may wish to meditate lying down. Or you may wish to speak to God out loud. Or, you may wish to raise your arms to heaven, as some saints used to do. You can't do this easily in a public place. As a result your meditation is inhibited from the start.

Jesus prayed in private places. The Gospel says that Jesus "departed to the mountain to pray." *Luke 6:12* And elsewhere it says that Jesus "went off to a deserted place, where he prayed." *Mark 1:35* Some meditation places you might try are—

- your bedroom,
- a little-used room in your house,
- any room after the family retires or before it rises in the morning.

The important thing about a meditation place is that it helps you pray better. The best way to determine the right place for you is through trial and error. Don't become discouraged if it takes a while to find "your" place.

When should you meditate?

Rising very early before dawn,
Jesus went off to a deserted place,
where he prayed.   Mark 1:35

A real estate man I know gets up early in the morning to pray; an aerospace engineer prays and reads Scripture on his lunch hour; a production manager of a computing firm prays after the children are in bed at night.   Ralph Martin

Some people don't like to schedule prayer. They prefer to pray or meditate when the mood strikes. That sounds good, but it does not always work out. The demands of modern life are such that if you don't schedule a time for meditating, you probably won't meditate.

When two people want to become better friends, they arrange times and places to meet. They don't leave their meetings to chance. The same is true when you want to deepen your friendship with God. Some popular meditation times are—

- after rising in the morning,
- during lunch break at noon,
- after returning home from work,
- at night just before retiring.

Again, finding "your" time may take a little experimentation, but it's worth the effort.

What posture should you use?

After . . . kneeling, Jesus prayed.   Luke 22:41

How much would you give for a formula that guaranteed to make you look younger, brighter, more attractive—and feel that way too? Probably a lot. Yet the secret is built right into the human body, your body. All you have to do is take a few minutes now and then to check up on your posture.   Warren Young

Posture is also important in meditation and prayer. Jesus prayed not only kneeling down but also lying down (Matthew 26:39). Some acceptable prayer postures are—

- sitting in a chair, back straight, feet flat on the floor,
- kneeling at a bedside,
- lying down,
- sitting cross-legged on the floor, back straight (possibly pressed against a wall), hands on knees.

This latter posture combines rest with alertness. It may take you a couple of weeks to get used to this posture, but the effort will be well worth it. Again, trial and error offer the best way to discover which posture helps you pray best.

Should you keep
a meditation journal?

Take a scroll and write on it
all the words I have spoken to you.   Jeremiah 36:2

A meditation journal is simply a daily record of the insights, feelings, or resolutions that occurred to you during your meditation. This record need not be long. A few sentences will do. For your convenience, *Challenge* provides a space for your daily record after each meditation.

Spiritual directors recommend a journal to beginners for various reasons. For example, a young man who had quit meditating for several weeks accidentally ran across his journal one day. He stopped what he was doing and began to read it. "Reading it," he said later, "inspired me to start meditating again." Here's a sample journal entry.

March 11, 8:00 A.M.

This morning I meditated sitting cross-legged on the floor. For me, this position is better than trying to meditate while lying on my bed.

During meditation I felt the desire to make up with someone I've been on the outs with for a long time.

How do you meditate?

"This is how you are to pray." Matthew 6:9

The procedure for meditating on the exercises in this book is always the same. It involves three steps:

1. *Preparation*—setting the stage for meditation
2. *Presence*—creating the climate for meditation
3. *Prayer* —meditating

Step one: Preparation

Begin by recalling the grace you seek through your meditation. This grace differs each week and is specified in the introduction to the week.

Next, read the Scripture passage that gives the theme of the daily meditation. After reading it, pause briefly to review it in your mind and to let it sink into your heart.

Next, read the story that develops the theme of the daily meditation. Again, pause to review it in your mind and to let it sink into your heart.

Lastly, *reread* the Scripture passage slowly and prayerfully. It is God's Word.

Step two: Presence

This step consists in putting yourself in God's presence. One way to do this is to close your eyes, relax your body, and monitor your breathing.

As you focus on your breathing, recall that breath points to God's presence within you. The Book of Genesis says, "The LORD God . . . formed a man . . . he breathed life-giving breath into his nostrils and the man began to live." *Genesis 2:7 (TEV)*

Breathing also points to the presence of the Holy Spirit within you. Jesus said to his disciples, " 'Peace be with you. As the Father sent me, so I send you.'

Then he breathed on them and said, 'Receive the Holy Spirit.' " *John 20:21-22 (TEV)*

If God makes his presence felt (for example, if you feel inner tranquility and peace), do not move on. Simply remain in a posture of openness and silent communication with God as long as it lasts—even if it is for the entire meditation period. Trying to *make* yourself feel God's presence, however, is almost always wrong. Feeling God's presence is a gift. If God wishes to give it to you, that is up to him. Your job is to keep your mind and heart open to God's will.

Step three: Prayer

Once you have placed yourself in God's presence, begin your reflection on the Scripture passage and the meditation story. To facilitate your reflection, a brief meditation guide has been placed at the end of each meditation story. The purpose of this guide is not to restrict your meditation, but to stimulate it. Use the guide or not, as you see fit.

Conclude your meditation by doing two things: (1) reread the Scripture passage prayerfully, and (2) speak to God from your heart, as the Spirit moves you.

One final point. Don't read ahead to see what is coming. Take each meditation exercise as it comes.

You are now ready to begin the exciting journey into the world of meditation. How exciting will it be? That depends on how courageous you are and how challenging God decides to be as you seek to deepen your relationship with the all-loving God.

1
YOU

Who are you?

I have called you by name. . . .
You are precious in my eyes.   Isaiah 43:1, 4

I've never met you. But I can tell you three things about yourself that even you may not know.

First, you're a special person. I know this because you're reading this book. It was probably recommended to you by someone, which makes you special, at least in that person's eyes. No one would recommend a book like this, except to a "special" person.

Second, you're a caring person. If you didn't care, you wouldn't be reading this book. You'd be doing something else. Only a caring person would take the time to read a book like this.

Finally, you're a daring person. When you accepted the challenge to make the meditation exercises in this book, you showed your willingness to plunge into the unknown. Only a daring person would do that. The meditations in this book could take you down paths you never dreamed you'd travel.

That brings us to the first week of meditations.

Someone said, "You are three persons: the one you think you are, the one other people think you are, and the one you really are."

This first week of meditations is designed to help you discover the *real* you. So the grace you ask for in each meditation is always the same:

Lord, help me see myself
as I *really* am.

Do one meditation a day. Spend no less than ten minutes and no more than twenty minutes on it. After each meditation take a few minutes to jot down four things in your journal entry:

1. The place you prayed

2. The time of day you prayed

3. The posture you used

4. The insights, etc., you received

Now begin. The disposition to have as you start is one of generosity. For each step you take toward God, God will take a dozen toward you.

Day one

What is man
that you should be mindful of him,
or the son of man
that you should care for him?
You have made him
little less than the angels.   Psalm 8:5–6

A college philosophy professor was walking along the street. His head was down and he was lost in meditation. Accidentally he bumped into an elderly lady. Instead of apologizing, he kept right on walking and meditating.

Enraged, the woman turned and shouted, "Who do you think you are, anyway?" Still deep in his meditation, the professor was heard to say, "Who am I? How I wish I knew!"

Funny as the incident is, it does leave us with a serious question—"Who am I?" Am I the creation of a loving God? Am I merely an accident of some blind force?

The famous astronaut John Glenn says a standard test for astronauts included the question "Who are you?" Candidates were asked to give twenty answers to that question. "The first few answers were easy," says Glenn. "After that, it got harder."

What answer would you give to the question "Who am I?" Why this answer? *Speak to God about any difficulty you may have in answering this question.*

_____

_____

_____

_____

_____

Day two

Then God said:
"Let us make man in our image,
after our likeness."   Genesis 1:26

The famous American cartoonist Thomas Nast was once at a party with some friends. Somebody suggested that he draw a caricature of each one present.

Using swift, bold strokes of his pencil, Nast made quick sketches of each of his friends. Then he passed them around for everyone to look at. There was a lot of laughter and joking. Then something unexpected happened. Everyone recognized everyone else, but few recognized themselves.

When it comes to ourselves, we seem to have a blind spot. We don't see ourselves as clearly as others see us. We don't recognize our main characteristics—our strengths and our weaknesses—as they really are.

There's a lot of truth in the saying, "If we saw ourselves as we *really* are, we would need an introduction."

What two words would you choose to describe yourself? Why these two words? *Speak to God about how he might describe you.*

_____
_____
_____
_____
_____
_____
_____
_____
_____

Day three

The LORD God formed man
out of the clay of the ground . . .
and so man became a living being.   Genesis 2:7

A wise old teacher gave this homework assignment to her students:

Find an unnoticed flower around your home and study it. Study its petals and leaves. Look at its colors. Turn it over and observe the underside of it. As you do, remember this is your flower. It might have gone unappreciated and unseen had you not found it and admired it.

The next day, after the students turned in their reports, the teacher said to them:

People are like your flower. Each one is unique. But you have to study them carefully to know this. So many people go unappreciated because no one takes the time to admire their uniqueness. Each of you is a masterpiece of God. There wasn't anyone like you before; there won't be anyone like you again.

What do you like most about yourself? What might God like most about you? *Speak to God about his answer.*

_____
_____
_____
_____
_____
_____
_____
_____
_____

Day four

*"Even the hairs of your head
have all been counted."*   Luke 12:7

They say the heads of blonds contain about
150,000 hairs; brunets, about 125,000; and redheads,
about 100,000.

It's difficult to verify how accurate this count is.
But the big numbers help us appreciate an example
Jesus used one day while addressing some down-
trodden people.

Pointing to a flock of sparrows, he said, "Are not
five sparrows sold for two small coins? Yet not one
of them has escaped the notice of God." Then,
walking over to a little girl, Jesus ran his fingers
through her hair and said with a smile, "Even the
hairs of your head have all been counted. Do not be
afraid. You are worth more than many sparrows."
Luke 12:6-7

Jesus assures the people that they are precious
in his Father's sight. His Father knows them and
values them more than they know and value
themselves. He treasures them beyond their wildest
imagining.

One answer to the question "Who am I?" is this:
"I am someone deeply valued by God."

What special talents do you have? How are you
using those talents now? *Speak to God about how you
could use your talents even more effectively.*

_____
_____
_____
_____
_____

Day five

*Each one must examine his own work . . .
without regard to someone else.*   Galatians 6:4

A woman was seated on a train, looking out of the window at the scenery. Suddenly she caught sight of a white cottage on a hillside. Against the background of the dark green grass, the cottage sparkled in the sun and was a lovely sight.

Months later the same woman was on the same train. But now it was winter, and sparkling white snow covered the countryside. The woman remembered the cottage and watched for it. This time it shocked her. Against the background of the sparkling snow, the cottage looked dirty and drab. Now it was far from lovely.

There's a lesson here. We tend to compare ourselves to people around us. The story of the little white cottage shows how misleading this can be. We can evaluate ourselves as being lovely or ugly, depending on the people around us.

If you don't evaluate yourself by comparing yourself to those around you, how do you evaluate yourself? *Speak to God about how he will evaluate you on Judgment Day.*

_____
_____
_____
_____
_____
_____
_____
_____

"Not as man does God see,
because man sees the appearance
but the LORD *looks into the heart."*   1 Samuel 16:7

The movie *Mask* is based on the true story of sixteen-year-old Rocky Dennis. He had a rare disease that made the bones of his face grow larger than they should.

As a result, Rocky's face was terribly misshapen. This made some people shy from him and others snicker at him. Through it all, Rocky never pitied himself. Nor did he give way to anger. He felt bad about his appearance, but he accepted it as a part of life.

One day Rocky and some friends were at an amusement park. They went into a "house of mirrors" and began to laugh at how distorted their bodies and faces looked.

Suddenly Rocky saw something that startled him. One mirror distorted his misshapen face in a way that made it appear normal. In that mirror Rocky was strikingly handsome. For the first time, Rocky's friends saw him as he was on the inside: a truly beautiful person.

What is the difference between your "inside self" and your "outside self"? *Speak to God about what he likes most about your "inside self."*

_____

_____

_____

_____

_____

_____

Day seven

*We know that when Christ appears,
we shall be like him.*   1 John 3:2 (TEV)

There's a legend about an Indian boy who found
an eagle's egg. He took the egg home and put it into
a chicken's nest. A baby eagle hatched out of the egg
and grew up with the other baby chickens.

The little eagle thought he was a chicken and did
what the other chickens did. He scratched in the dirt
for seeds and ate insects. He made chicken noises and
thrashed his wings awkwardly, rising only a few feet
off the ground.

Time passed and the eagle got bigger. One day
he saw a magnificent bird soaring high in the sky
above him. It glided on the wind in great circles.

"What a marvelous bird!" the eagle said to an
adult chicken standing nearby.

"That's an eagle," said the adult chicken. "It's
the king of the birds. But don't get any silly ideas.
We could never be like him or do what he's doing."

How is this story a parable of Jesus and you? *Talk
to God about how you can start to become more fully the
person he made you to be.*

_____

_____

_____

_____

_____

_____

_____

_____

_____

_____

2
ACCEPTING YOURSELF

Do you rejoice in who are you?

By the grace of God I am what I am.
1 Corinthians 15:10

Two women named Hooker wrote letters to syndicated columnist Ann Landers.

The first woman resented her name. The second reacted just the opposite, saying she rejoiced in it.

The second woman said that a sense of humor about her name has made all the difference. "When I'm introduced and someone snickers, I say, 'Yes, the name is Hooker—as in happy.' "

When she receives crude phone calls asking how much she charges, she replies, "More than you can afford, Buddy!"

"Believe it or not," she says, "there are advantages to being a Hooker. Your name is rarely misspelled, and no one ever forgets it."

The reaction of the two women typifies the reaction people have to the "negative" things about themselves that they can't change. They either resent them, or they accept them and rejoice in them.

21

This second set of meditation exercises is designed to help you accept yourself totally and to rejoice in who you are. Thus the grace (petition) you ask for before each exercise is always the same:

Lord, help me accept myself
and rejoice in who I am.

As you do each exercise, be faithful to the three steps described under "How do you meditate?" on pages 7–8. (You might wish to keep a marker there for handy reference.) After your prayer, be sure to record these four things in the space provided after each meditation:

1. The place you prayed
2. The time of day you prayed
3. The posture you used
4. The insights, etc., you received

Day one

We know
that in all things God works for good
with those who love him.   Romans 8:28 (TEV)

Robert Bruce was walking along a crowded street. Suddenly he heard someone singing. It wasn't loud singing, but more like someone singing to himself. Bruce looked around and found the source. It was a young man in a wheelchair, pushing himself along with the only useful limbs he had: his arms.

Consider another example. A young girl named Golda was depressed because she was not beautiful. But as she grew older, her attitude changed. She says:

I realized that not being beautiful was a blessing in disguise. It forced me to develop inner resources. I came to understand that women who can't lean on their beauty [must work harder and] . . . have the advantage.

Golda Meir went on to become the first woman prime minister of Israel. Like the young man in the wheelchair, she not only accepted herself but rejoiced in who she was.

What do you find hard to accept about yourself? Why this? *Speak to God about why you find this hard to accept.*

_____

_____

_____

_____

_____

_____

_____

_____

Day two

*I have the strength for everything
through him who empowers me.*   Philippians 4:13

Tom Dempsey was born without a right hand and with only half a right foot. But that didn't stop him from playing football in junior college. He got so good as a place kicker that the New Orleans Saints signed him.

On November 8, 1970, the Saints were trailing Detroit 17–16 with two seconds to go on Detroit's forty-five-yard line. The Saints' coach, J. D. Roberts, tapped Tom on the shoulder and said, "Go out there and give it your best shot!"

The holder set the ball down eight yards behind the line, instead of seven, to give Tom a split second more time to get the ball off. That put the ball sixty-three yards from the uprights.

The rest of the story is history. Tom broke the NFL field goal record by seven yards. He told *Newsweek* magazine later: "I couldn't follow the ball that far. But I saw the official's arms go up and I can't describe how great I felt."

To what extent do you let obstacles or handicaps control you? *Speak to Jesus about how he faced up to obstacles and dealt with them.*

Day three

"Knock and the door will be opened to you."
Matthew 7:7

When Glenn Cunningham was seven years old, his legs were so severely burned that doctors considered amputation. At the last minute they decided against it. One of the doctors patted Glenn's shoulder and said, "When the weather turns warm, we'll get you into a chair on the porch."

"I don't want to sit. I want to walk and run, and I will." There was no doubt in Glenn's voice. The doctor walked away.

Two years later Glenn was running. The boy was not running fast, but he was running.

Eventually Glenn went to college. His extracurricular activity was track. Now he was running not to prove the doctors wrong, but because he was good at it. Soon intercollegiate records began to crumble beneath his driving legs. Then came the Berlin Olympics. Glenn not only qualified and ran in them, but also broke the Olympic record for the 1,500-meter race.

The following year, Glenn broke the indoor mile record. The boy who wasn't supposed to walk again became the world's fastest human.

What are some obstacles in your life? Do you have faith that God will help you deal with them? *Speak to God about why your faith may be lacking.*

_____
_____
_____
_____
_____

25

Day four

*"Whoever wishes to come after me
must deny himself, take up his cross,
and follow me."* Mark 8:34

James Du Pont of the Du Pont Company recalls an episode that happened to him when he was seven years old.

He awoke one night out of a sound sleep. His mother was sobbing loudly. It was the first time he'd ever heard her cry. Then he heard his father speaking to her. Du Pont says:

My dad's voice was low and troubled as he tried to comfort mother—and in their anguish they both forgot about the nearness of my bedroom. I overheard them.

Describing the effect this experience had on him, Du Pont says:

While their problem . . . has long since been solved and forgotten, the big discovery I made that night is still right with me. Life is not all hearts and flowers. It's hard and cruel . . . much of the time.

When did you learn firsthand that life can be cruel and hard? *Speak to Jesus about how he dealt with the hardness and cruelty of life.*

Day five

*The hard trials that come
will not hurt you.*   Isaiah 43:2 (TEV)

Near Cripple Creek, Colorado, gold and tellurium occur mixed as telluride ore. The refining methods of the early mining camps couldn't separate the two elements. So the ore was thrown away.

One day a miner mistook a lump of ore for a lump of coal and tossed it into his stove. Later, while removing ashes from the stove, he found them littered with tiny gold beads. Picking up one of the beads, he checked it closely. He couldn't believe his eyes. The bead was pure gold. The heat had burned away the tellurium, leaving the gold in a purified state. The discarded ore was reworked and yielded a fortune.

There's an important lesson here. We are like telluride ore. People throw us away, thinking we have no value. But inside of us is pure gold. It often takes some trial in the fiery furnace of affliction, however, to bring it out of us.

Recall a time in your life when some tragedy or cross turned out to be a blessing in disguise. *Speak to God about the purpose of life's tragedies and crosses.*

_____

_____

_____

_____

_____

_____

_____

_____

_____

_____

Day six

*"Blessed are you who are poor,
for the kingdom of God is yours."*   Luke 6:20

Newsweek magazine notes that you'll find works of Marc Chagall "in cathedrals, synagogues and opera houses from New York to Paris to Jerusalem." Some critics call him the greatest artist of the twentieth century.

In his book *My Life,* Chagall tells how he grew up in a poor Jewish family in Russia. His interest in art was aroused one day when he watched a classmate copy a picture from a magazine. Shortly afterward, when his mother was baking bread, he touched her flour-smeared elbow and said, "Mama, I want to be an artist."

Chagall's dream eventually took him to Paris, where he won worldwide acclaim.

Chagall never forgot his poverty. In fact, he rejoiced in it and felt that it helped him become an artist. He wrote:

The very worst thing to have too early is a little success, a little money . . . a little satisfaction. The little satisfactions . . . hold you back from big dedication.

Do you believe God can turn such things as poverty and illness into something good for a person? *Speak to God about these things.*

Day seven

"A sower went out to sow."   Mark 4:3

An old Arab saying reads, "I will set my face to the wind and scatter my seeds on high."

That's a poetic way of saying that God expects us to use our talents (seeds) to build a better world. It also warns us that we will encounter difficulties (wind) as we strive to do this. Consider this example.

A young man was dying from a fatal disease. Shortly before he died, he wrote:

We have to believe that every part of our lives has value. What has value can be shared. So I have something to share . . . even though I am in a hospital unable to leave my room. . . .

The only answer I have so far is to embrace every situation . . . with confidence in its meaning and value. . . . I really think that is what Jesus meant when he called us the light of the world. . . . He wants us to believe in our meaning and value. To believe in him and his Father, we have to believe in ourselves.

How fully do you accept yourself in your situation in life? *Speak to Jesus about any difficulty you have in doing this.*

_____

_____

_____

_____

_____

_____

_____

_____

_____

3
YOUR LIFE

How meaningful is your life?

*"I came so that they might have life
and have it more abundantly."*   John 10:10

Jerry Kramer played for the Green Bay Packers and made the All-Pro team four times. During his career he kept a diary. Later it was published under the title of *Instant Replay: The Green Bay Diary of Jerry Kramer.*

In an entry for November 26, Jerry talks about the movie *Cool Hand Luke.* It's about a wild character who was in and out of prison all of his life. The last time Luke escaped from prison, he went into an old church, knelt down, and said something like this: "Old Man, whadaya got planned for me? What's next? Whadaya put me on earth for?" Commenting on the scene, Kramer writes:

I ask myself the same questions. I often wonder where my life is heading, and what's my purpose here on earth besides playing the silly games I play every Sunday. I feel there's got to be more to life than that. There's got to be some reason for it. . . . I didn't come

31

up with any answers this morning. I just thought about it for a while.

The meditation exercises for this week focus on the meaning of life. Thus the grace you ask for before each exercise is this:

Lord, teach me the meaning of life.

Once again, be faithful to the three steps described under "How do you meditate?" on pages 7–8. This cannot be stressed enough. If you are still experimenting with a time, place, or posture, continue to list it in your journal entries. If not, discontinue listing it.

One final word. Some people find it rewarding to use a shortened version of the Scripture passage that introduces each daily meditation as a way of extending that meditation into their day. For example, the passage that introduces "Day one" of this week could be shortened to "Where from? Where to?" These four words could be written on a slip of paper, placed on your desk (or whatever), and repeated during the day. Give it a try for a few weeks. It could be immensely rewarding.

Day one

*"Where have you come from
and where are you going?"* Genesis 16:8

King Edwin lived in seventh-century England. One day he was talking to a close friend about the shortness of life. His friend make this comparison:

O king, recall the room where you meet with your officers on cold winter nights in front of the huge fireplace. During those meetings, a lone sparrow sometimes flies into the room through an opening, exiting just as quickly through another opening.

Life is like the swift flight of that sparrow. While it is inside the room, safe from the cold, it enjoys a brief space of fair weather. But then it vanishes again into the night. No one knows whence it came or where it goes.

So it is with us, O king. Our time on earth is brief, like the flight of that sparrow through the meeting room. No one knows whence we came or where we go.

If someone asked you where you came from and where you are going, what would you reply? *Speak to God about your answer.*

Day two

Teach us to number our days aright,
that we may gain wisdom of heart.   Psalm 90:12

In the Pulitzer prize winning stage play *Our Town,* young Emily dies giving birth to her first child. She sits on the stage in the world of the dead. On the other side of the stage, in the world of the living, the funeral party has just buried Emily and is leaving the cemetery.

Later Emily learns from the dead that it is possible for her to choose one day from her life and relive it. But they all advise against it. Emily ignores their advice and chooses to relive one of the happiest days of her life, her twelfth birthday.

She begins. But before she gets half way through the day, she cries out, "I can't. I can't go on. It goes so fast. We don't have time to look at one another. Take me back—up the hill—to my grave."

Then, with a heavy heart, she asks one of the dead, "Do humans ever realize life while they live it?—every, every minute?"

The dead person pauses a minute and says sadly, "No. The saints and poets, maybe—they do some."

Do you tend to live in the fast lane, forgetting to stop and smell the flowers now and then? *Speak to God about how you might slow down to do this.*

34

*"They look but do not see
and hear but do not listen or understand."*
Matthew 13:13

Starbuck is the name of a character in the play *The Rainmaker*. He's terribly unhappy with life but doesn't know why. Another character, named Lizzie, says it's his own fault. She says he never pauses long enough to look at life and to see it as it really is.

Then Lizzie gives him an example. She says that sometimes when she's doing the dishes in the kitchen, she watches her father playing cards with her brothers. At first, she sees only a middle-aged man, not very attractive or interesting to look at. But as she continues to look, she begins to see other things.

I'll see little things I never saw in him before. Good things and bad things—queer little habits I never noticed he had—and ways of talking I never paid any mind to. And suddenly I know who he is—and I love him so much I could cry! And I want to thank God I took the time to see him real.

_____

What keeps you from pausing to discover life and people as they really are? *Discuss this question with Jesus.*

_____
_____
_____
_____
_____
_____
_____
_____

Day four

*"Do not seek what you are to eat
and what you are to drink. . . .
Your Father knows you need [these things].
Instead, seek his kingdom,
and these other things will be given you."*
Luke 12:29–31

A motorist drove into a "full-service" station. Three attendants charged out to meet him. The first washed the windows; the second checked under the hood; the third checked the tires. When they finished, the motorist paid for the ten gallons of gas and drove off.

Three minutes later he returned. Once more, the three attendants charged out. "I'm embarrassed to ask you this," said the motorist, "but did anyone put gas in my car?" The attendants looked at one another. In their rush to serve, they had forgotten the gas.

This humorous incident is a good picture of what happens to us, sometimes. We get so involved in living life that we forget why God gave us life. We never stop long enough to ask ourselves if what we are planning to do with our life is what we really ought to do with it.

———

What is one thing you have thought about doing with your life? Why this? *Speak to God about what he would like you to do with your life.*

Day five

*"Whoever loses his life for my sake
and that of the gospel will save it."* Mark 8:35

There's a movie star in John O'Hara's novel *The Last Laugh*. He has been an SOB all of his life. Eventually his career goes into a tailspin, and he ends up a complete zero.

Realizing his situation, he says to himself, "At least I was once the idol of movie fans all over the country. Nobody can take that away from me." When you read this, you feel like laughing out loud and saying, "Big deal, buster! Who cares now!"

*To every man there openeth
A way and ways and a way.
And the high soul climbs the high way,
And the low soul gropes the low,
And in between, on the misty flats,
The rest drift to and fro.
But to every man there openeth
A high way and a low.
And every man decideth
The way his soul shall go.* John Oxenham

If your life continues in its present course, what way of life will you have chosen—the high, the low, or the middle? *Speak to Jesus about the course of your present life.*

Day six

> *"What profit is there
> for one to gain the whole world
> and forfeit his life?"*   Mark 8:36

A basketball team had just celebrated a prayer service before playing in the state tournament. During the service, the chaplain said to the team, "The important thing ten years from now won't be whether or not you won the state championship. Rather, it will be what you became in the process of trying to win it."

After the service, when the chaplain returned to the sacristy to take off his vestments, he heard the coach say to the players:

Sit down a minute. Our chaplain said something that is bothering me. I wonder what we've become in the process of trying to put together a winning season. Have we become more loyal to ourselves and one another? More loving? More committed? Have we learned to put the team's welfare ahead of our own interests? Have we become better Christians?

I hope to God that we have. I pray to God that we have. Because if we haven't, we've failed God; we failed our families and friends; we've failed ourselves.

Take to heart the coach's words. *Speak to Jesus about how they apply to your life.*

_____

_____

_____

_____

_____

_____

_____

Day seven

*I am now giving you the choice
between life and death . . .
and I call heaven and earth
to witness the choice you make.*
Deuteronomy 30:19 (TEV)

On the night of April 15, 1912, the *Titanic* hit an iceberg and sank, taking over 1,500 lives.

Seventy years later a magazine recalled the terrible disaster and asked its readers a shocking question: "If you'd been present on the *Titanic* when it was sinking, would you have rearranged the deck chairs?"

At first we say to ourselves, "That's a silly question. No sane person would ignore the shouts of drowning people and go about rearranging the deck chairs on a sinking ship."

But as we read further, we see the reason for the strange question. And we end up asking ourselves, "Are we, perhaps, rearranging the deck chairs on a sinking ship?"

For example, are we so caught up in the material side of life that we are ignoring the spiritual side of life? Are we so concerned about our own interests in life that we are ignoring the plight of other people, and forgetting why God gave us life?

How would you answer these questions? *Speak to God about your answers.*

_____

_____

_____

_____

_____

_____

4
GOD

Who is God?

"Who are you, sir?"   Acts 9:5

The movie *Laura* concerns a young detective who is called in to solve the murder of a beautiful young woman. One night someone knocked at Laura's apartment door and then killed her by firing a shotgun into her face.

For the next few days, the detective spends all of his time in Laura's apartment, checking everything she owns. He even reads her personal diary, trying to find a clue that might lead to her murderer.

Then something strange happens. The detective finds himself becoming emotionally involved. He finds himself falling in love with Laura. He finds himself falling in love with a dead person.

One night he's in Laura's apartment pondering the case. Suddenly a key turns in the lock. The door opens, and there stands Laura.

To make a long story short, the slain woman was someone who had used the apartment while Laura was away for a week.

41

The movie ends with Laura and the detective falling in love, marrying, and living happily ever after.

The movie *Laura* acts as a modern parable of what God wants to happen to each of us. God wants us to study the world around us and, through its beauty, to discover the Creator. God also intends that our story end the same way that the movie ends. God intends that we fall in love with the Creator and live happily ever after with him.

The meditation exercises for this week are designed to help you do just that. They are designed to help you discover God, fall in love with God, and live happily ever after with God. Thus the grace (petition) you ask for in each exercise is this:

Lord, help me know and love you better.

During the next seven days, make a special effort to place yourself in God's presence. Keep in mind, however, that trying to make yourself *feel* God's presence is nearly always wrong. A sensible awareness of God's presence is a gift from God. All you can do is to open your heart to receive it.

Day one

Where were you when I founded the earth?   Job 38:4

A woman sent this anonymous poem to Ann
Landers in response to someone who had written Ann
that all believers are simpletons:

Oh you who could not put one star in motion,
Who could not build one mountain out of earth,
Or trace the pattern of a single snowflake
Or understand the miracle of birth,

Presumptuous mortal
who cannot alter the universe in any way,
Or fashion one small bud, release one raindrop
Or toss one cloud into a sunny day,

Oh earthling who could never paint a sunset
Or cause one dawn to shine.
Oh puny man who cannot create a single miracle,
How dare you doubt the only one who can.
Author unknown

Small wonder Albert Einstein wrote that any
serious scientist "becomes convinced that a spirit is
manifest in the laws of the Universe—a spirit vastly
superior to that of man, and one in the face of which
we with our modest powers must feel humble."

When you look at the world around you, do you
see what the poet saw? Do you see what Einstein
saw? *Speak to God about what you see.*

Ever since the creation of the world,
his invisible attributes
of eternal power and divinity
have been able to be understood and perceived
in what he has made.
As a result, they have no excuse.   Romans 1:20

The film *Lawrence of Arabia* deals with the life of Colonel T. E. Lawrence, the British army man. Lawrence spent a long time among the Arabs.

A Western scholar once bragged to an Arab about the power of the telescope. The Arab listened carefully. When the scholar stopped talking, the Arab said to him, "You Westerners see millions of stars and nothing else. We Arabs see only a few stars—and God."

Helen Keller, who was deaf and blind, made a similar observation. She said:

I walk with people whose eyes are full of light but who see nothing in the sea or the sky. . . . It is far better to sail forever in the light of blindness . . . than to be content with the mere act of seeing.

Are you one of the people of whom Jesus said, "They shall indeed look but never see. . . . They have closed their eyes"?   Matthew 13:14-15 *Speak to Jesus about this.*

Day three

Oh LORD, *our Lord,*
how glorious is your name over all the earth!

Psalm 8:1

A father took his young son on a camping trip
in the Adirondack Mountains in New York. To make
the trip more enjoyable, he hired an experienced guide
to accompany them. The guide led them off the beaten
trails and took them into the heart of the great forest.

The boy was amazed at how the old guide spotted
things that the ordinary person missed. One day, after
the guide had been pointing out some hidden beauties
in the forest, the boy exclaimed, "I'll bet you can even
see God out here!" The old guide replied, "Son, it's
getting hard for me to see anything else but God out
here."

The old guide's remark reminds us of the words
of the poet E. B. Browning:

Earth's crammed with heaven,
And every common bush afire with God.
But only he who sees takes off his shoes;
The rest sit round it and pluck blackberries.

When was the last time you paused long enough
to watch a sunset or to listen to a bird's song? *Ask*
God to give you eyes to see him more clearly in nature.

_____

_____

_____

_____

_____

_____

_____

Day four

"Remove the sandals from your feet,
for the place where you stand
is holy ground." Exodus 3:5

In his book *The Golden String,* the British writer Bede Griffiths describes an episode that took place when he was a schoolboy.

He was walking outside one summer evening. As he strolled along by himself, he became aware of how beautifully the birds were singing. He wondered why he had never heard them sing like this before.

As he continued to walk, he came upon some hawthorn trees in bloom. They were lovely and gave off a sweet fragrance that filled the air. Bede wondered why he had never noticed this beauty or fragrance before.

Finally, he came to a field. Everything was quiet and still. As he stood there, watching the sun disappear below the horizon, he felt inclined to kneel on the ground. It was as though God were there in a tangible way.

"Now that I look back on it," wrote Griffiths, "it seems to me it was one of the decisive moments of my life."

What was one of the most memorable moments in your life? *Speak to God about what made it special.*

_____
_____
_____
_____
_____
_____
_____

Day five

*"I say to you, when you did not do
for one of these least ones,
you did not do for me."* Matthew 25:45

After the great Japanese Kagawa found Christ, he left his comfortable home and went to live in the slums of Tokyo. There he shared himself and his possessions with the poor and needy.

In his book *Famous Life Decisions,* Cecil Northcott says that Kagawa eventually gave away all his clothing, keeping only a tattered kimono. On one occasion, even though sick, he continued to preach to people in the rain, repeating over and over, "God is love! God is love! Where love is, there is God."

William Barclay gives us an insight into the heart and mind of Kagawa when he quotes the great man as saying:

God dwells among the lowliest. . . . He is there with beggars. He is among the sick, he stands with the unemployed. Therefore let those who would meet God visit the prison cell before going to the temple. Before they go to church, let them visit the hospital. Before they read the Bible, let them help the beggar.

If you are having trouble finding God, could it be you are looking for him in the wrong places? *Speak to God about his presence in our world.*

47

Day six

God is wise in heart and mighty in strength;
who has withstood him and remained unscathed?

God made the Bear and Orion, the Pleiades and
the constellations of the south; he does great things past
finding out, marvelous things beyond reckoning. . . .
Should he pass by, I am not aware of him; should he
seize me forcibly, who can say him nay? Who can say to
him, "What are you doing?" . . . I could not believe
that he would hearken to my words. Job 9:9–12, 16

God is beyond human comprehension. The
greatest blunder we continue to make is to try to
reduce God to the level of human definition. Saint
Augustine put it this way:

God is inexpressible. It is easier for us to say what
he is not than what he is. . . . If we would conceive of
him, we would conceive of something other than God.
He is not at all what we have conceived him to be.

And Mohandas Gandhi put it this way:

God is that indefinable something which we all feel,
but which we do not know.

How do you feel God's presence in your life?
Speak to God about any difficulty you have in feeling
his presence.

_____
_____
_____
_____
_____
_____
_____

Day seven

Hearken to my words, O LORD,
attend to my sighing.   Psalm 5:2

An eleventh-century monk, Anselm of Canterbury, wrote a beautiful book called *Proslogion*. It was designed to help unlearned people find God. The book contains this prayer:

O Lord my God,
teach my heart where and how to seek you,
where and how to find you. . . .
You are my God and you are my Lord,
and I have never seen you.
You have made me and remade me,
and you have bestowed on me
all the good things I possess,
and still I do not know you. . . .
I have not yet done that
for which I was made. . . .

Teach me to seek you . . .
for I cannot seek you unless you teach me
or find you unless you show yourself to me.
Let me seek you in my desire,
let me desire you in my seeking.
Let me find you by loving you,
let me love you when I find you.

How earnestly are you seeking God? If you were searching for your own father or mother, would you do so more eagerly than you are now searching for God? *Speak to God about this.*

5
GOD AND YOU

How do you experience God?

I know someone in Christ
who, fourteen years ago . . .
was caught up to the third heaven . . .
and heard ineffable things,
which no one may utter.   2 Corinthians 12:2-4

The life of astronaut Jim Irwin was changed forever after his voyage to the moon aboard *Apollo 15.* Irwin writes in his book *To Rule the Night:*

I wish I had been a writer or a poet, so that I could convey adequately the feeling of this flight. . . . It has been sort of a slow-breaking revelation for me. The ultimate effect has been to deepen and strengthen all the religious insight I ever had. It has remade my faith. . . . On the moon the total picture of the power of God and his Son Jesus Christ became abundantly clear to me.

What happened to Jim Irwin must happen to all of us. There comes a time in our lives when we must bring God down out of the sky and let him enter into our everyday life. We must discover God as someone who is close to us, closer than our own breath. We must experience God as someone who knows us and loves us better than we know and love ourselves.

The meditation exercises for this week are designed to help you do just that. They are designed to help you discover God as someone who knows and loves you deeply. Thus the grace you ask for in each exercise this week in this:

Lord, help me discover
how deeply you know and love me.

A word about distractions. Now that you have meditated for a few weeks, you have no doubt experienced times when your mind and your heart wander off as you are meditating. What should you do when this happens? Saint Francis de Sales gives this reply:

Bring your wayward heart back home quietly. Return it tenderly to its Master's side. If you did nothing else during prayer but return your heart continually and patiently to the Master's side, your time of prayer would be well spent.

Day one

I sought the LORD, and he answered me.   Psalm 34:5

We might compare meditation or prayer to a television set. An example will illustrate.

The air space in the room in which you are sitting is alive with hundreds of television shows. They swirl about invisibly in living color and exciting sound. This is not science fiction; it's science fact.

But the only way you can prove this fact is by means of a "big dish" and a television set. Here's where the comparison with prayer comes in.

Just as the air space around you is alive with an invisible television world, so it is alive with an invisible faith world. And just as the way to get in touch with the invisible television world is by means of a television set, so the way to get in touch with the invisible faith world is by means of prayer.

In other words, prayer is the way we enter into contact with the most ultimate of all realities, the reality of God and the invisible world of faith.

What do you find easiest about prayer? Hardest about prayer? *Speak to Jesus about how you might improve your prayer.*

_____

_____

_____

_____

_____

_____

_____

_____

_____

I am the LORD, your God,
who grasp your right hand;
it is I who say to you,
"Fear not, I will help you."   Isaiah 41:13

One night Dr. Martin Luther King was in bed. He was about to doze off when the phone rang. A voice on the other end said, "Listen, nigger, we've taken all we want from you. Before next week, you'll be sorry you ever came to Montgomery."

Dr. King hung up. Suddenly all his fears came crashing down on him. He got up and heated a pot of coffee. Then he sat down at the kitchen table, bowed his head, and prayed:

People are looking to me for leadership, and if I stand before them without strength and courage, they too will falter. I am at the end of my powers. I have nothing left. I've come to the point where I can't face it alone.

At that moment, Dr. King felt the personal presence of God in his life as he had never felt it before. His strength and courage returned, and he went on to change history.

In time of need do you turn to God for help as confidently as a child turns to a parent? *Speak to God about how you might build your confidence in his help.*

_____
_____
_____
_____
_____
_____

Day three

*Nothing will be able to separate us
from the love of God.*   Romans 8:39

A stanza from an old hymn describes God's love in these poetic words:

*The love of God is greater far
Than tongue and pen can ever tell;
It goes beyond the highest star.*

But the most moving stanza of the hymn is the last one. James Montgomery Boice says this stanza was not written by the original composer, but added later. Found on the wall of a room in a mental hospital, it reads:

*Could we with ink the ocean fill
And were the skies of parchment made;
Were every stalk on earth a quill,
And every man a scribe by trade;
To write the love of God above
Would drain the ocean dry;
Nor could the scroll contain the whole,
Though stretched from sky to sky.*

What keeps you from giving God the same place in your heart that he holds in the universe? *Speak to Jesus about the place he gave God in his own heart.*

Day four

"Know that I am with you."   Genesis 28:15

Thor Heyerdahl believed that South Americans could have reached Polynesia on ocean currents. Guided by ancient drawings, he built a raft called *Kon Tiki,* and navigated it across the 4,300-mile distance.

Oddly enough, Thor once had a deathly fear of water. He overcame it when a boat carrying him capsized near a waterfall in a Canadian river. As the rapids swept him along toward the falls, a strange thought entered his mind. He would soon learn which of his parents was right about God and life after death. His father was a believer; his mother was not.

Then something strange happened. The words of the Lord's Prayer came to his mind and he began to pray. Suddenly a burst of energy surged through him. He began to battle the rapids. Soon he was keeping pace with them. Some unseen power was helping him. A few minutes later he made it to shore.

That day on the Oxtongue River, Thor lost his fear of water and gained something else as well—a sure knowledge that his father was right.

———————

Have you ever experienced God's help in a similar situation? Did it change you as much as it changed Heyerdahl? *Speak to God about this.*

_____

_____

_____

_____

_____

_____

_____

Day five

You know when I sit and when I stand.   Psalm 139:2

Eddie Rickenbacker and a crew of seven crashed
into the Pacific. They survived twenty-one days by
eating fish they caught, drinking rain water, and
praying. Here's a prayer they repeated often:

O LORD . . . you know me;
you know when I sit and when I stand;
you understand my thoughts from afar.
My journeys and my rest you scrutinize,
with all my ways you are familiar.
Even before a word is on my tongue,
behold, O LORD, you know the whole of it.

Behind me and before, you hem me in
and rest your hand upon me.
Such knowledge is too wonderful for me;
too lofty for me to attain.
Where can I go from your spirit?
From your presence where can I flee? . . .

If I take the wings of the dawn,
if I settle at the farthest limits of the sea,
even there your hand shall guide me,
and your right hand hold me fast. . . .
I give you thanks . . . ;
wonderful are your works.   Psalm 139:1–14

Do you really believe God knows you better than
you know yourself? That he loves you more than you
love yourself? *Speak to God about this mystery.*

*"Whoever loves me will keep my word,
and . . . we will come to him
and make our dwelling with him."* John 14:23

A little girl was standing with her grandfather by an old-fashioned open well. They had just lowered a bucket to draw some water to drink. "Grandfather," asked the little girl, "where does God live?"

The old man picked up the little girl and held her over the open well. "Look down into the water," he said, "and tell me what you see." "I see myself," said the little girl. "That's where God lives," said the old man. "He lives in you."

The grandfather was right. Jesus said to his disciples, just before he died: "I will not leave you orphans; I will come to you. . . . On that day you will realize that I am in my Father and you are in me and I in you." *John 14:18, 20*

Likewise, Paul wrote: "Do you not know that you are the temple of God, and that the spirit of God dwells in you?" *1 Corinthians 3:16-17*

Why do you find it hard to believe that the God who created the universe lives within you? *Talk to God about this mystery.*

_____

_____

_____

_____

_____

_____

_____

_____

Day seven

When you pass through the water,
I will be with you.   Isaiah 43:2

Roger Bolduc died after a long bout with cancer. He resigned himself to this and accepted it as a gift from God. Just before his death, he wrote:

God has become so real. . . . I feel that he loves me more than ever. . . . I can feel his power—it's always there . . . . I feel loved.

Some time after Roger died, an old priest told a friend:

Someday we're going to realize that God loves us with a father's love, only infinitely more so. When that realization dawns on us, it will change our lives in a way that we never dreamed possible.

The old priest had a marvelous insight. God loves us more than we love ourselves. That incredible truth is just waiting to explode in our tiny hearts. When it does, we'll never be the same again.

Why do you find it hard to believe that God loves you with an infinite love? *Talk to God about this as a child would talk to a loving parent.*

6
GOD'S PLAN

What is God's plan for you?

I know well
the plans I have in mind for you . . .
plans to give you a future full of hope.   Jeremiah 29:11

In his book *I Believe,* Coach Grant Teaff of Baylor University in Texas describes an incident that happened earlier in his coaching career.

One Saturday night his football team was flying back to Texas. Suddenly the plane developed trouble. The pilot shouted for them to prepare for a crash landing. Minutes later the plane bellied across the ground. A shower of sparks engulfed it. Miraculously, however, it didn't explode and no one was hurt.

Later, Teaff knelt down in the team's dressing room and prayed:

God, I know that you have a plan, a purpose, and a will for my life and the lives of these young men. I do not know what it is, but I'll . . . try to impress upon the young men I coach this year and forever that there is more to life than just playing football; that you do have a purpose for our lives.

61

This week's meditations are designed to help you realize that God made you for a purpose. So the grace you seek in each exercise in this:

Lord, help me realize
that you created me for a purpose.

A word about meditation and discouragement. Some people become discouraged after a few weeks of meditation. They expect certain things to happen, but their expectations aren't fulfilled.

We shouldn't approach meditation with any expectancies. An example will illustrate. Did you ever bite into something in the dark, thinking it was one thing when it was another? The shock of the unexpected taste surprised you so much that you almost spit it out.

Meditation can be like that. Approach it with preconceived ideas, and it may disappoint you. Approach it without preconceived expectations, and it will delight you abundantly in its own special time and way.

Meditating is like planting seeds. You may not see the results immediately, but eventually the acorn grows into a great tree.

Day one

In you I trust.
Show me the way in which I should walk.
Psalm 143:8

Doug Alderson wrote a fascinating article in *Campus Life* magazine, describing his two-thousand-mile hike down the Appalachian Trail. Doug had just graduated from high school and had lots of unanswered questions: Was there a God? What was the purpose of life? What should he do with his life? Doug wrote:

There had to be more to life than money, TV, parties, and getting high. . . . My hike was a search for inner peace, a journey to find myself.

The long hours on the trail gave Doug a chance to get to know himself better. When he returned home five months later, he was a different person. Even his dog eyed him strangely, as if to say, Where have you been? What have you done? You look different.

Doug was different. He had found what he was searching for. There was a God, life had a purpose, and he had a role to play in it.

What are some unanswered questions in your life? *Speak to God about one of these questions.*

_____
_____
_____
_____
_____
_____
_____
_____

Day two

*Let us love not in word or speech
but in deed and truth.*   1 John 3:18

Gale Sayers, who played for the Chicago Bears in the 1960s, was one of the greatest running backs of all time. Around his neck he wore a gold medal. On it were inscribed three words: "I Am Third."

Those words became the title of his best-selling autobiography. The book explains why the words meant so much to Gale. They were the motto of his track coach, Bill Easton, back at the University of Kansas.

Coach Easton kept them on a plaque on his desk. One day Gale asked him what they meant. Easton replied, "The Lord is first, my friends are second, and I am third."

In Gale's second year with the Bears, he decided he wanted to wear something meaningful around his neck. So he bought a gold medal and had the words "I Am Third" engraved on it. Gale is the first to admit that he doesn't always live up to the motto. But wearing it around his neck, he says, keeps him from straying too far from it.

Would you be willing to wear Gale's medal around your neck and make its words your motto? *Speak to God about what changes you would have to make in your present life if you did this.*

Day three

*"I . . . chose you and appointed you
to go and bear fruit."*   John 15:16

There's an old Jewish legend that explains why God chose Moses over the other people on earth to lead his people, Israel.

One day Moses was shepherding some sheep that belonged to his father-in-law, Jethro. Suddenly he spotted a lamb darting off into the underbrush.

Moses dropped everything and pursued it, lest it become lost or killed by a wild animal. He finally caught up with the lamb at a tiny stream of water, where it was drinking feverishly.

When it had finished, Moses scooped it up in his arms, saying, "Little one, I didn't know you ran away because you were so thirsty. Your tiny legs must be tired." With that he placed the lamb on his shoulders and returned it to the flock.

Seeing how caring Moses was, God said, "At last I've found the special person I've been searching for. I will make Moses the shepherd of my people, Israel."

If you asked God about your present concern for other people, what might he say? *Talk to God about his answer.*

_____

_____

_____

_____

_____

_____

_____

_____

*An argument arose among the disciples
about which of them was the greatest.*   Luke 9:46

The sculptor Donatello was a contemporary of the great sculptor Michelangelo. One day Donatello rejected a block of marble because it was too flawed for him to use. The workmen took the same block to Michelangelo.

When Michelangelo inspected it, he saw the same flaws. But Michelangelo also saw the block as a challenge to his skill. He accepted it and proceeded to carve from it *David,* one of the world's most prized treasures of art.

The disciples of Jesus were like that block of marble. They, too, were flawed. The Gospel even shows them jockeying for places of honor in the kingdom of God.

A lesser leader than Jesus would have rejected the disciples, just as Donatello rejected the flawed block of marble. But Jesus didn't do that. He accepted them, flaws and all, and proceeded to carve from them the foundation upon which he built his Church.

Do you believe that God accepts you, flaws and all? Do you believe that God can make something beautiful out of you in spite of your flaws? *Speak to God about his plan for you.*

_____
_____
_____
_____
_____
_____
_____

Day five

*"If you have faith
the size of a mustard seed,
you would say to [this] mulberry tree,
'Be uprooted and planted in the sea,'
and it would obey you."*   Luke 17:6

In the movie *The Empire Strikes Back,* Luke Skywalker flies his X-wing plane to a swamp planet. There he seeks out a guru named Yoda to teach him to become a Jedi warrior. Luke wants to free the galaxy from its oppression by the evil tyrant Darth Vader.

Yoda agrees to help Luke and begins by teaching him how to lift rocks with his mind.

Then, one day, Yoda tells Luke to lift his X-wing plane out of the swamp water. Luke complains that lifting rocks is one thing, but lifting planes is quite another. When Yoda insists, Luke makes a valiant effort but fails.

Yoda then takes over and lifts the plane with ease. Luke exclaims, "I don't believe it!" Yoda replies, "That's why you couldn't lift it, because you didn't believe."

———————

How is the scene between Yoda and Luke a good picture of God and you? *Speak to God about why you may be less willing to commit yourself than Luke was.*

_____
_____
_____
_____
_____
_____
_____

Day six

Trust in the LORD with all your heart.   Proverbs 3:5

A young man had a profound experience of God. Afterward he knelt down and committed his life to God, totally. As he did, he suspected that his life would now become hard and painful. Just the opposite happened. God blessed the young man beyond his wildest dreams.

Eventually, each of us must come to the same realization that the young man did. John Henry Newman expressed it this way:

God has committed some work to me
which he has not committed to another.
I have a mission—
I may never know it in this life,
but I shall in the next. . . .

Therefore I will trust him.
He does nothing in vain.
He may prolong my life,
he may shorten it;
he knows what he is about. . . .
O my God, I will put myself
without reserve in your hands.

How firmly do you believe that God has committed some special work to you? *Speak to God about what this work may be.*

_____

_____

_____

_____

_____

_____

Day seven

"Do not be afraid; just have faith."   Mark 5:36

Imagine that you are about to be born into the world. God calls you into his presence and offers you two lives on earth to choose from.

God's first choice involves a short life of sickness, poverty, and ridicule by people. This is the best way you can accomplish the task God has in mind for you.

God's second choice is just the opposite. It involves a long life of health, wealth, and honor.

Realizing what a difficult decision he is presenting to you, God asks you if you want to spend a few days thinking about it before giving your final answer. On the other hand, God wants you to be totally honest. Would thinking about it for a few days be merely a formality, because you would probably choose the second option anyway?

Note, God is not asking you to choose now. God is merely asking you if you'd be willing to think seriously about accepting his first choice.

What response would you make to God? *Speak to God about why you made this choice.*

_____
_____
_____
_____
_____
_____
_____
_____
_____
_____

7
PRINCIPLE
AND FOUNDATION

What is your reaction to God's plan?

I have set before you life and death,
the blessing and the curse. Choose life.
Deuteronomy 30:19

There's a humorous story about a man and a woman who were shipwrecked on a deserted island for ten years. One day a ship spotted their smoke signal and dispatched a lifeboat to the site.

But instead of rescuing the couple right away, the crew handed them some newspapers, saying, "The captain wants you to read these and see what's going on in the world before you decide whether you want to be rescued."

If you're like most people, there are times when you'd like to flee civilization and go off to a deserted island. But you know you can't. God put you in this world to make it a better place. Now it's up to you to decide what you'll do. You can't sit on the sideline and be a spectator. You must decide.

The goal of this week's meditations is to make you aware of the personal price you'll have to pay if you decide to say yes to God's plan for you. So the grace you ask for in each meditation is this:

Lord, help me see the price I must pay
if I say yes to your plan.

The meditation exercises for this week are tremendously important. You may wish to seek God's special help by performing some extra service for others or by making some personal sacrifice—like not eating between meals this week. This is merely a suggestion. Do whatever the Spirit moves you to do.

Now begin, keeping in mind that this week is especially important. Give it your best shot.

Day one

*"Your light must shine before others,
that they may see your good deeds
and glorify your heavenly Father."* Matthew 5:16

Before the age of electricity, city streets were lit by gas lamps. Lamplighters went about every night lighting the lamps with a flaming torch.

One night an old man was seated at a window in his house. Across the valley was a street on a hillside. There he could see the torch of a lamplighter lighting lamps as he went. Because of the darkness, however, he could not see the lamplighter. He could see only his torch and the trail of lights it left behind.

After watching for a few minutes, the old man pointed to the trail of lights and said to a friend standing next to him:

That lamplighter is a good example of how Christian men and women should live. You may never have known them. You may never have met them. You may never have even seen them. But you know that they passed through the world by the trail of lights they left behind.

_____

What trail of lights are you leaving behind you? *Speak to God about the need to illuminate the darkness in our world.*

_____
_____
_____
_____
_____
_____
_____
_____

73

Day two

We journeyed through impassable deserts,
but the way of the LORD we knew not.   Wisdom 5:7

Kim and Amy were walking down the street discussing religion. Suddenly they came upon a gang. Kim saw her chance to deliver a telling blow to Amy's faith. Pointing her finger at the toughs, she said, "Look, Amy, it's been two thousand years since Jesus came into the world to save us from unsavory characters like that. But they still run wild on our streets. If Jesus came to rid our world of evil, why are there still so many vicious people?"

Five minutes later, the two young women came upon a group of children. Their faces and hands were covered with dirt.

Now Amy had a chance to reply. Pointing a finger at the dirty children, she said, "Look, Kim, it's been two thousand years since soap was discovered. Why are there still so many dirty children running around?"

Why is there so much evil in the world after two thousand years? What are you doing about it? *Speak to Jesus about what more you could do.*

_____

_____

_____

_____

_____

_____

_____

_____

_____

Day three

"Whoever remains in me and I in him will bear much fruit." John 15:5

A woman was touring a piano factory. First, the guide showed her a large warehouse room where workers were busy sawing and shaping rough wood.

Next, the guide took the woman into a room where workers were building frames.

Then, the guide took the visitor into a room where people, wearing face masks, were carefully sanding and varnishing piano frames.

Next, the woman visited a room where a few skilled technicians were assembling metal strings and ivory keys into the frames.

Finally, the guide led the woman into the showroom, where a musician was seated at a piano playing incredibly beautiful music.

Afterward the woman thought to herself:

The difference between what I saw in the warehouse room and the showroom is the difference between an acorn and a tree. It's the difference between what I am now and what God intends that I become.

Do you really believe God made you to sing a special song to the world? *Speak to God about the song he wants you to sing.*

_____
_____
_____
_____
_____
_____
_____
_____

Day four

*"The kingdom of heaven
is like a treasure buried in a field
which a person finds . . .
and sells all that he has
and buys that field."* Matthew 13:44

A magazine ran a story about teenagers who belong to the Santa Clara Swimming Club. Every morning they get up at 5:30 and hurry through the chilly air to an outdoor pool. There they swim for two hours. After a shower and a bite to eat, they dash off to school.

After school they return to the pool for two more hours. Then they hurry home, eat, hit the books, and fall into bed, exhausted. The next morning the alarm rings at 5:30, and they start all over again. When asked why she sacrifices so much to swim, one girl said:

My goal is to make the Olympic team. If going to parties hurts that, then why go? There is no such thing as too much work. The more miles I swim, the better. Sacrifice is the thing.

This story raises a question: If these kids are willing to sacrifice so much for the Olympics, what are we willing to sacrifice to carry out God's plan to build a better world?

How would you answer that question? *Speak to God about your answer.*

Day five

"Take up his cross daily and follow me."   Luke 9:23

Years ago Dr. Lloyd Judd practiced medicine in rural Oklahoma. Many people in that area were poor and had no transportation to come to his office. So he often had to drive to their homes to treat them.

One day Dr. Judd took sick. He checked into a hospital and discovered that he had terminal cancer. His thoughts turned to his young children. He had much to tell them, but they were too little to understand. So he recorded a set of tapes, which his children could play back when they got older. One of the tapes deals with choosing a career in medicine. Dr. Judd said to his children:

Are you willing to get out of a warm bed on a cold night and drive twenty miles to see a sick person, knowing that they can't pay you and that they could wait until morning to be treated? If you can say yes to that question, you are ready to study medicine.

———————————

Could you say yes to Dr. Judd's question? How willing are you to serve above and beyond the call of duty? *Speak to Jesus about this.*

_____

_____

_____

_____

_____

_____

_____

_____

_____

_____

_____

Day six

How shall I make a return to the LORD
for all the good he has done for me? Psalm 116:12

The Spiritual Exercises of St. Ignatius present a theology or "First Principle and Foundation" for living one's life. It goes like this:

I believe that God created me to share my life and love with him and other people, forever. I believe that God created all other things to help me achieve this lofty goal.

I believe, therefore, that I should use the other things God created insofar as they help me attain my goal and abstain from them insofar as they hinder me. It follows, therefore, that I should not prefer certain things to others. That is, I should not value, automatically, health over sickness, wealth over poverty, honor over dishonor, or a long life over a short one.

I believe my sole norm for valuing and preferring a thing should be this: How well does it help me attain the end for which God created me?

Would you be willing to adopt Saint Ignatius' theology or "First Principle and Foundation" as the guiding norm for your own life? If not, reword it to make it acceptable. *Speak to God about it.*

Day seven

"Blessed are they
who hunger and thirst for righteousness,
for they will be satisfied."   Matthew 5:6

This anonymous meditation was found in the pocket of a dead Confederate soldier:

I asked for health,
that I might do greater things;
I was given infirmity,
that I might do better things. . . .
I asked for riches, that I might be happy;
I was given poverty, that I might be wise. . . .
I asked for power,
that I might have the praise of men;
I was given weakness,
that I might feel the need for God. . . .
I asked for all things that I might enjoy life;
I was given life, that I might enjoy all things.
I got nothing I asked for—
but everything I hoped for.
Almost despite myself,
my unspoken prayers were answered.
I am among all men most richly blessed.

Reread this meditation slowly, pausing after each thought to reflect on it. *Speak to Jesus about how it applies to your life.*

_____

_____

_____

_____

_____

_____

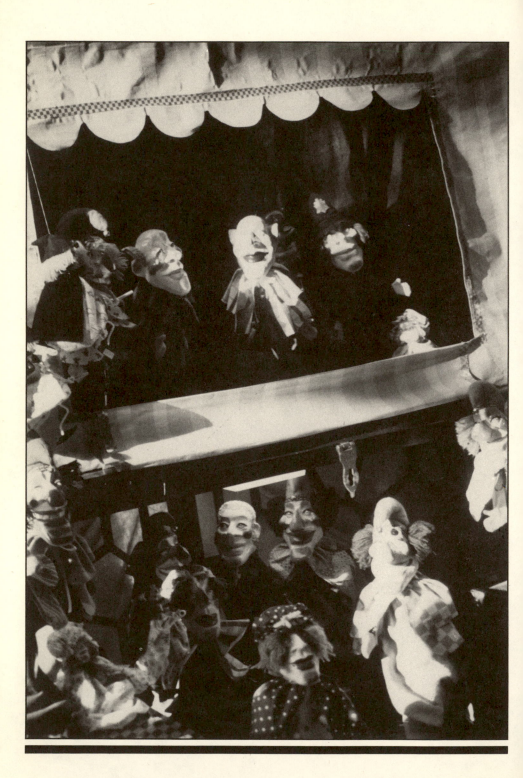

8
SIN

How aware are you of sin's power?

We journeyed through impassable deserts,
but the way of the LORD we knew not.   Wisdom 5:7

Someone compared people on earth to the images of people on a television screen. These tiny images owe their existence to the television set. When the set goes on, they go on. When the set goes off, they go off.

Suppose these images decided to rebel. Suppose they said to the television set, "We declare our independence from you; we don't need you. We can get along without you."

Such a situation would be ludicrous. It would be like an echo saying to a voice, "I declare my independence from you. I don't need you anymore."

In a sense that's what sin is. It's people on earth saying to God, "We declare our independence from you. We don't need you anymore." To put it in another way, sin is people, like you and me, saying no to God and to God's plan for us.

The meditations that follow deal with sin, the enemy of God's plan. They put us in touch with the destructive power of evil. They show how sin is an affront to God and how it frustrates God's plan for us. Sin also destroys ourselves and our world. The grace you ask for in each meditation is the following:

Lord, help me see and be appalled by
the destructive power of sin.

Conclude each meditation by reciting the Lord's Prayer (Our Father) in a low, audible voice. Pause after each thought to let it sink in. Give special attention to the final words of the prayer:

Forgive us our trespasses
as we forgive those who trespass against us,
and lead us not into temptation,
but deliver us from evil.

Day one

My sins so overcome me that I cannot see.
Psalm 40:13

Years ago there was a popular television program called "The Mork and Mindy Show." Mork was an alien who had remarkable power.

One day he shared some of this power with a few of his friends on earth. Touching his fingertips to theirs, he transferred just a little bit to them. Right away they began using it to make people do ridiculous things, like turn cartwheels and leap up and down. Mork was horrified and shouted, "Stop! You're misusing the power. Give it back!"

That episode is a good illustration of what sin is. It's misusing the power God gives to us.

Here is another example. The news media carried an incredible story about a supersonic jet fighter plane that shot itself down. It had fired a burst of shells, but because the plane was traveling at such a high speed, it accidentally dove right into the path of its own shell fire.

Again, that's what sin is. It's having the power of God within us, but using it to shoot ourselves down.

If you asked God to evaluate your overall use of his gifts, might he give you a passing grade? *Speak to God about your failure to use his gifts better.*

_____

_____

_____

_____

_____

_____

Day two

Consider your ways!   Haggai 1:5

Sin is hard to define. Some people define it as "a deliberate breaking of God's law."

Others say this definition is too impersonal. Sin involves more than the breaking of God's law. More to the point, it involves the breaking of God's friendship. It's saying no to God and to God's plan for us.

But even this definition does not tell the whole story. It is still inadequate. It can give the wrong impression that sin occurs only when God is the direct target of our rejection.

Jesus' description of the Last Judgment shows that God can be rejected in ways far more subtle than most of us would like to admit. Jesus put it this way:

"Lord, when did we see you hungry or thirsty or a stranger or naked or ill or in prison, and not minister to your needs?" He will answer them, "Amen, I say to you, what you did not do for one of these least ones, you did not do for me."   Matthew 25:44-45

How do you look upon sin in your life? *Contemplate the Christ on the cross and then come to a definition of sin.*

When the L*ord* *saw
how great was man's wickedness on earth . . .
he regretted
that he had made man on the earth.*   Genesis 6:5–6

Some time ago *Time* magazine carried a disturbing news story. It told how the Detroit Zoo was forced to increase its number of guards. The reason for the beefed-up security was not to protect people from animal attacks, but to protect animals from people attacks.

In recent years a growing number of animals have been brutalized by zoo spectators.

For example, an Australian wallaby was stoned to death by rock-throwing youths.

A pregnant reindeer had a miscarriage when rowdies bombed the mother with firecrackers, sending the frantic animal into convulsions.

And in still another case, visitors amused themselves by dropping cigar butts on the backs of alligators. Then when the butts burned through the skin of the reptiles, causing them to writhe in pain, the visitors roared with laughter.

How do you explain such irresponsible behavior? *Speak to Jesus about what you, personally, might do to help combat it.*

_____
_____
_____
_____
_____
_____
_____

Day four

Fear and trembling come upon me,
and horror overwhelms me. Psalm 55:6

Martin Gray was born in Warsaw in 1939, when the Nazis invaded Poland. He grew up when the infamous ghetto wall was built around the Jews of Warsaw. Later, at Treblinka, he helped carry bodies to mass graves.

Martin describes all these things in his book *For Those I Loved.* It's a moving story of how he tried to convince himself, at first, that these things were not really happening.

Men do not play "catch" with babies and then drop them on concrete. Men do not rip open the stomachs of pregnant women. Men do not herd other human beings into cattle cars. Men do not execute other men, by the thousands, in gas chambers.

But that's precisely the point of Gray's book. "Men" do not do those things, but "men" can turn into savage beasts.

Gray also makes another disturbing point. The Nazis were not the only beasts. The people who looked the other way were also beasts in their own way.

Could something like this happen today—even to you? *Speak to God about how you can make sure this doesn't happen—especially to you.*

Day five

*They trample the heads of the weak . . .
and force the lowly out of the way.*   Amos 2:7

You'd hardly expect the dean of American psychiatry to stand up and talk about sin. But that's what Dr. Karl Menninger does in his book *Whatever Became of Sin?*

Dr. Menninger is deeply troubled by individuals who won't admit to personal sins. But he's even more troubled by "sins of collective responsibility," that is, sins committed by groups of individuals or by entire nations of people.

What kind of sins, specifically, does Dr. Menninger have in mind? Citywide disregard of the ghetto poor, nationwide pollution of the environment, industry-wide exploitation of migrant workers—these are just a few of the "collective sins" that scare him. The tragic thing about these "collective sins" is that single individuals, like you and me, don't consider themselves responsible or guilty in any way.

Dr. Menninger's words make us ask ourselves about our responsibility concerning such sins, no matter how indirect or marginal.

What collective sins might you be participating in? *If you asked God what you could do about your involvement in these sins, what might he say to you?*

_____

_____

_____

_____

_____

_____

_____

Day six

Defend the lowly . . . ; render justice
to the afflicted and the destitute.   Psalm 82:3

The Mountain People is a disturbing book about a vanishing African tribe. As you read it you ask yourself, "Can the true story of the Ik tribe teach us something about ourselves?" You answer, "Probably not!"

At first glance you'd seem to be right. Driven from their hunting grounds, the Ik are barely surviving. They have become selfish. "Every man for himself" has become their motto.

Food is so scarce that young people steal from the mouths of the elderly. Along with the sick and the weak, the elderly are simply ignored and left to die. Love and kindness, as we know them, have vanished.

The author of *The Mountain People,* Colin Turnbull, sees a parallel between what has happened to the Ik and what is happening to Western society. Like the Ik, we have opted to travel the road of selfish individualism. Our primary driving force is our own self-interest.

Turnbull ends his book on a chilling note. He asks, "Is the sorry plight of the Ik a preview of our own future in the West?"

What is the primary driving force in your life? *Speak to Jesus about the primary driving force in his life.*

Day seven

Who will deliver me from this mortal body?
Romans 7:24

Lord of the Flies is the story of a group of fourteen-year-old English schoolboys. They become marooned on a deserted island when a plane evacuating them from war-torn England crash-lands in the Pacific Ocean. The pilot and copilot are killed outright, but the boys emerge unharmed.

At first, things go well. The boys enjoy the adventure of exploring the island. They also enjoy the excitement of setting up their own society and making their own rules.

But, gradually, their lives turn sour. Bickering breaks out and the boys split into two rival camps. Then they turn savage and start killing one another. Fortunately, a British warship spots them on the island and saves them from annihilating themselves.

The irony appears when the boys board the warship, whose crew is also involved in the wartime annihilation of human beings.

Author William Golding ends his story with this eerie question: "The adults rescued the children, but who will rescue the adults?"

How would you answer Golding's question? *Speak to God about the hostility in our world and what his followers—you—might do about it.*

9
SENSE OF SIN

How aware are you of personal sin?

Peter fell at the knees of Jesus and said,
"Depart from me, Lord,
for I am a sinful man." Luke 5:8

A mother had a small baby girl who was unable to feel pain because of a defect in her nervous system.

One day the mother heard her daughter laughing and cooing in the next room. Checking on her, she found the child had chewed on the tip of her finger and was amusing herself by drawing patterns with the blood dripping from it.

The loss of our sense of pain is similar to the loss of our sense of sin. John Connery, who writes on this subject, says our sense of sin is linked to our sense of God. The closer we are to God, the more aware we are of our sinfulness.

On the other hand, the farther we are from God, the less aware we are of our sinfulness. This is because our distance from God reduces the contrast necessary for us to recognize our true condition. Connery concludes by saying that the loss of a sense of sin is as tragic as the loss of physical pain.

The meditations that follow deal with the "sense of sin." They try to make us aware of the alarming degree of sinfulness that is present in our lives. The grace you ask for in each meditation is the following:

Lord, give me an awareness
of my own sinfulness in your sight.

Again, conclude each meditation by reciting the Lord's Prayer in a low, audible voice. Pause after each thought to let it sink in. Give special attention to the final words of the prayer: "Forgive us our trespasses as we . . . "

In the course of this week's meditations, it might be appropriate for you to celebrate the sacrament of Reconciliation. You may even feel moved to want to make a "general confession" of your entire life. If you do, ask a priest or your spiritual director how to go about doing this. Many people find this sacramental encounter to be a tremendously peace-filled and joyful experience.

Day one

Set your heart aright.   Job 11:13

"Airwolf" was a television series in the early 1980s. Jan-Michael Vincent, who costarred in it, told a *TV Guide* reporter, "I feel like I've given the show a real shortchange. I don't feel I've given 25 percent."

When asked if this was because he didn't like his role in the series, the actor drawled, "No, I was just lazy."

Consider another example. A traveling salesman was working in a rural area. One day he came upon a farmer sitting in a rocking chair on the porch of a rundown house. After introducing himself, he launched into his pitch, saying, "Sir, I have a book that's worth its weight in gold. It describes how to farm your land ten times better than you're doing now."

The farmer continued to rock. Then, after a long pause, he said, "Young feller, I already know how to farm my land ten times better than I'm doing now. My problem isn't knowing what to do. It's doing it."

We can all relate to the stories of Vincent and the farmer. We are all guilty of failing to do what we ought to do.

———————

Do you sin by omission (not doing what you ought) more than by commission (doing what you ought not to do)? *Speak to Jesus about where you need to improve most.*

Day two

As a body is one . . . so also Christ.
1 Corinthians 12:12

A music critic received a last-minute concert assignment and had to cancel dinner with a friend. An hour later the daughter of the concert's soloist was killed in a car accident, forcing the concert's cancellation.

The critic phoned her friend. "Good news!" she said. "The soloist's daughter was just killed, so they've canceled the concert." Suddenly the critic realized what she had said. The death of the young woman was not "good" news; it was "tragic" news.

How often do we find ourselves in a position similar to the music critic's? We are so concerned about our own tiny world that we lose sight of the bigger world. We are so fixated on our own petty interests and pleasures that we become blind to the crying needs of others. We forget what Paul didn't want us ever to forget:

As a body is one . . . so also Christ. . . .
If one part suffers,
all the parts suffer with it.   1 Corinthians 12:12, 26

How guilty are you of focusing on yourself and not seeing the needs of others? *Speak to Jesus about how you might open your eyes and heart more fully to others' needs.*

_____
_____
_____
_____
_____

Day three

*If we say, "We are without sin"...
we make God a liar.*   1 John 1:8, 10

The worst evil isn't sinning. It's sinning and denying it. Happy are we if we can admit to our faults. Woe to us if we sin and then refuse to admit it in order to stay virtuous in our own eyes. It's better to commit a sin than to corrupt a principle.

Louis Evely has a lot more to say about this in his book *In His Presence*. He writes:

You will repent of a straightforward sin more easily than one wrapped in doubt. Don't muddy the water so as to fish from it whatever you desire, pretending all the while it happened by chance.

Then in a burst of emotion, Evely says:

Commit straightforward, clear-cut and undeniable sins of which you will later be able to repent with the same sincerity you use in committing them. . . . If you are weak enough to sin, do not be too proud to recognize the fact.

How honest and straightforward are you about your own sinfulness? *Speak to Jesus about any problem you may have in this regard.*

Day four

Take to heart these words. Deuteronomy 6:6

If you get what you want
in your struggle for self,
And the world makes you king for a day,
Just go to the mirror and look at yourself,
And see what that man has to say.

For it isn't your father, or mother, or brother,
Who upon you their judgment will pass.
The fellow whose verdict counts most in your life
Is the one staring back from the glass. . . .

He's the fellow to please—
never mind all the rest!
For he's with you right up to the end.
And you've passed
your most difficult dangerous test,
If the man in the glass is your friend.

You may fool the world down the pathway of years,
And get pats on the back, as you pass,
But your final reward will be headache or tears,
If you've cheated the man in the glass.

Author unknown

Meditate on this poem verse by verse. *Speak to God after meditating on each verse.*

_____

_____

_____

_____

_____

_____

_____

_____

Day five

*A clean heart create for me, O God,
and a steadfast spirit renew within me.*   Psalm 51:12

Thomas Merton had just graduated from high school and was touring Europe alone. His father had died the year before, and Tom was leading a wild life.

One night in his room, he underwent a soul-stirring experience. It made him deeply aware of all the sinfulness in his life. He wrote later in *The Seven Storey Mountain:*

I was filled with horror . . . and my whole being rose up in revolt and horror with what was within me, and my soul desired escape . . . from all this with an intensity and urgency unlike anything I had ever known before.

And now I think for the first time in my whole life I really began to pray . . . praying to the God I had never known, to reach down towards me out of his darkness and help me to get free of the thousand terrible things that held my will in their slavery.

Have you ever had an experience like this? *Speak to Jesus about what steps you might take to rout out the sinfulness from your life.*

_____

_____

_____

_____

_____

_____

_____

_____

_____

_____

Day six

Upon him was the chastisement
that makes us whole,
by his stripes we were healed.   Isaiah 53:5

We all need to admit two things to ourselves. First, that we are sinners. Second, that in spite of this, our Father in heaven loves us. Julian of Norwich, the great English mystic, explains that even past sins can be turned into something good, if we acknowledge them as sins. Julian says, for example:

If we never fell, we should never know how weak and wretched we are in ourselves; nor should we appreciate the astonishing love of our Maker. . . . We sin grievously, yet despite all this . . . we are no less precious in his sight. By the simple fact that we fall, we gain knowledge of what God's love means.

Julian's words are a beautiful illustration of what Paul means when he says, "All things work for good for those who love God."   *Romans 8:28*   Julian would add to Paul's words, "Yes, even in sin."

How ready are you to admit your sinfulness? *Speak to God about how he can even bring good out of it.*

Day seven

My sins so overcome me
that I cannot see . . .
and my heart fails me.   Psalm 40:13

Replay in your imagination what went on in the minds and hearts of the first woman and the first man after they sinned. Visualize all the suffering that their sin unleashed in the world—not merely in the ancient world, but also in our modern world.

Pass in review all the people who have sinned since the time of the first sin. Consider how their sins have added to the suffering of the world.

Stand appalled at what sin is: not only an affront to a loving God but also an instrument of suffering and destruction.

Imagine Jesus hanging on the cross and suffering with incredible pain. Speak to him and ask him why he, God's own Son, decided to take flesh and die for our sins—your sins. Then ask yourself these three questions?

What have I done for Christ?
What am I doing for Christ now?
What ought I to do for Christ in the future?

How would you answer these questions? How might Jesus answer these questions for you? *Speak to Jesus about this.*

_____

_____

_____

_____

_____

_____

_____

10
FUTURE JUDGMENT

How will God evaluate your life?

For we shall all stand
before the judgment seat of God.   Romans 14:10

One day a shabbily dressed man was standing on a busy Chicago street corner. As office workers filed by on their way to lunch, he'd suddenly raise his arm, point at the one nearest him, and shout, "Guilty!"

Then without expression, he'd resume his stiff stance for a few seconds before repeating the gesture and making the solemn pronouncement again— "Guilty!"

The effect on the office workers was almost eerie. They would glance at the man, look away, glance back, and hurry on.

Humorous as the story is, it makes an important point: We're all guilty of sin and will someday have to stand judgment before God. The meditations that follow deal with this fact. The grace you ask for is the following:

Lord, help me live in such a way now
that I'll rejoice in your judgment later.

Spiritual directors recommend a daily "judgment" of one's actions. One way to do this is to take three minutes each night to do the following:

First minute. Replay your day. Pick out a *high* point—a good thing you did, like helping someone in need. Talk to God about it. End by thanking God for inspiring you to do it.

Second minute. Replay your day again. This time pick out the *low* point—a bad thing you did, like hurting a loved one. Talk to Jesus about it. Then ask Jesus to forgive you.

Third minute. Look ahead to tomorrow to a *critical* point—a hard thing you must do, like making up with someone. Talk to the Holy Spirit about it. Then ask the Holy Spirit to help you deal with the situation.

Beginning tonight, set aside three minutes each night to "judge" your day. Use the trinitarian model above, or a similar one.

Day one

There's a novel called *The Man Who Lost Himself*. In it the hero trails a suspect to a Paris hotel. To learn the suspect's room number without arousing suspicion, the hero gives the desk clerk his own name and asks him if a man by that name is registered. While the clerk checks the room list, the hero plans to watch for the other man's name and room number.

To the hero's utter surprise, the clerk doesn't check the register. He simply says, "Yes, he's in room 40, and he's expecting you." Well, the hero is amazed and has no choice but to go. He follows the bellhop to room 40.

When the door opens, he can't believe his eyes. Standing before him is a man who is his exact double, except that he's heavier and about twenty years older. The man turns out to be the hero himself, twenty years in the future.

The story is pure science fiction, but it contains an important truth: There's a person in the future waiting for each one of us. It's the person we ourselves will be ten or twenty years from now.

What will that person be like? *Speak to Jesus about what changes you might make so that you can be prouder of that person.*

When they sow the wind,
they shall reap the whirlwind.   Hosea 8:7

John was a building contractor for a construction company. His specialty was large luxury homes.

To increase his income, John routinely cheated on the materials that went into the homes. He was so clever at concealing these shortcuts that he joked to a close friend that even he couldn't detect his own shortcuts.

Sometimes his cheating reached such a proportion that the homeowners were in fairly serious danger because of the underconstructed electrical systems and the like.

The building contractor's shortcuts were especially dangerous in the final home he built. Even he worried about some of the things he did in that home.

You can imagine his utter consternation, therefore, when the company gave the contractor this home as a retirement gift. It would be the home in which he and his wife would spend the rest of their years.

How is this story a parable of life? What corners are you cutting in your life, figuring nobody will be the wiser for it? *Speak to God about the shortcuts in your life.*

_____
_____
_____
_____
_____
_____
_____

Day three

Each one may receive recompense,
according to what he did in the body,
whether good or evil.   2 Corinthians 5:10

In an ancient play called *Everyman,* God sends Death to Everyman to tell him his life is over.

When Everyman recovers from shock, he asks Death to give him a few minutes to ask his friends Money, Fame, and Power to accompany him on the journey. Death obliges, but each friend refuses. In the end, only one person agrees to accompany him: Good Works.

When death comes for us, no friend will go with us into the next life except Good Works.

There's a plaque in London that pays tribute to a certain Charles Gordon. It reads:

> *To the memory of Charles Gordon*
> *Who at all times and everywhere gave*
> *His Strength to the Weak*
> *His Substance to the Poor*
> *His Sympathy to the Suffering*
> *His heart to God*

If you died tonight, what one thing would you be most proud of? Least proud of? *Speak to Jesus about these things.*

_____
_____
_____
_____
_____
_____
_____
_____

Day four

"He has kept watch over my sins. . . .
They have settled about my neck,
he has brought my strength to its knees."
Lamentations 1:14

There's a moving story that has survived the centuries. It's about Pietri Bandinelli, an attractive young man who used to sing in the Milan cathedral choir. He had beautiful, clear eyes and a kind face.

According to the story, Leonardo da Vinci chose Bandinelli to be his model for Jesus in his painting *The Lord's Supper.*

Years later Leonardo still had not completed the painting. One day, however, the spirit moved him, and he went out into the slums of Milan to look for a model for Judas. After a few hours he found the perfect man. His eyes were shifty and clouded; his face had a hardened look.

Later, while the man was posing, Leonardo paused and asked him, "Have we met before?" There was a long silence. Then the man broke it, saying, "Yes, I was your Jesus model years ago, but much has happened in my life since then."

What lesson does this story hold for you? *Speak to God about your desire to live out his plan for you.*

_____
_____
_____
_____
_____
_____
_____
_____

Day five

Do you suppose . . . that you will escape the judgment of God? Romans 2:3

In April 1987, Hall of Famer Mickey Mantle was returning by plane to his home in Dallas. Suddenly he began to sweat and have difficulty breathing. The thought flashed into his mind: "I'm having a heart attack!" He summoned a flight attendant and was given oxygen. When the plane landed, he was rushed to a hospital.

Later, Mantle told an Associated Press correspondent about a dream he had while he was in the hospital.

"I dreamed I died and went to heaven. Saint Peter greeted me. I said, 'I'm Mickey Mantle.' He said, 'Really? Come in, God wants to see you.'

"I went in to see God, and he said, 'We can't keep you here because of the way you acted. But do me a favor and sign six dozen baseballs.' "

When the humor of Mantle's dream subsides, truth emerges: No one will escape God's judgment, and no one will get VIP treatment in that judgment.

What frightens you most about standing before God in judgment? *Speak to God about this fear, and ask him how you can overcome it.*

Some people's sins are public,
preceding them to judgment. 1 Timothy 5:24

Dr. Wilder Penfield heads up the Neurological Institute in Montreal. One day while operating on a patient under local anesthesia, he made an amazing discovery. *Time* magazine reported it this way:

Montreal surgeon Wilder Penfield . . . by chance found brain sites that when stimulated electrically led one patient to hear an old tune, another to recall an exciting childhood experience in vivid detail, and still another to relive the experience of bearing her baby.

Dr. Penfield's discovery convinces some scientists that every action of our life is recorded in our brain. More than that. Our feeling about these actions at the time we did them is also recorded. In other words, there's solid physiological support for the biblical teaching of a personal last judgment.

"I'll tell you a secret," said the French novelist Albert Camus. "Do not wait for the last judgment. It is taking place every day."

What is Camus's point? *Speak to Jesus about his current judgment of your life.*

_____

_____

_____

_____

_____

_____

_____

_____

Day seven

*All the dead were judged
according to their deeds.*   Revelation 20:13

In Westminster Abbey there's a tiny chapel called Saint George's Chapel. It's a memorial to Londoners killed in World War II air raids.

Inside the chapel are four large books containing the names of over 60,000 air-raid victims. One book lies open, and on it shines a light illuminating the page of names.

Each day the page is turned, revealing a new set of names. As you look at them, you have no way of knowing whether the person whose name you are reading was rich or poor, young or old, handsome or ugly. Nor does it matter. All that matters is what each person became in the course of his or her life.

In her book *Saint-Watching,* Phyllis McGinley says:

When I was seven years old I wanted to be a tight-rope dancer and broke my collarbone practicing on a child's-size high wire. At twelve I planned to become an international spy. At fifteen my ambition was the stage. Now in my sensitive declining years I would give anything . . . to be a saint.

How have your ambitions changed with time? *Speak to God about what it means to be a saint.*

_____
_____
_____
_____
_____
_____
_____

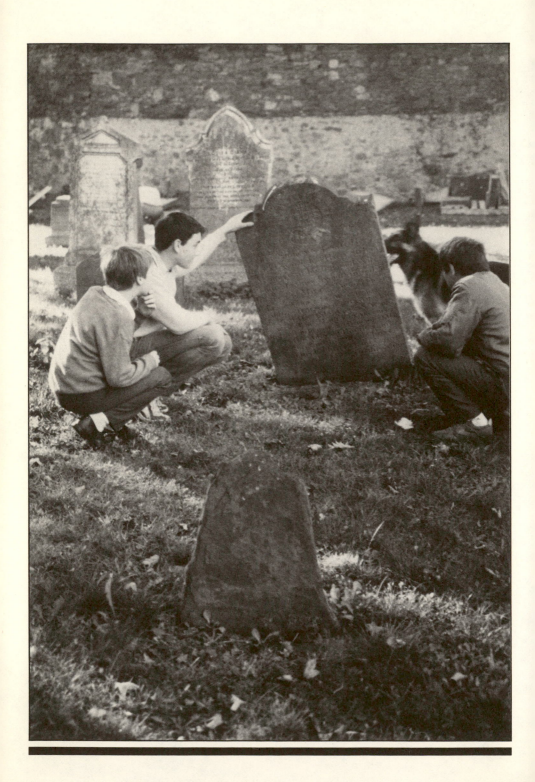

11
DEATH

Are you ready to say yes to death?

There is an appointed time
for everything. . . .
A time to be born, and a time to die.
Ecclesiastes 3:1–2

The famous French aviator Antoine de Saint-Exupéry was forced down in the Sahara, a thousand miles from civilization.

Repairing his damaged engine, with one eye on his vanishing water supply, Saint-Exupéry came face-to-face with death. Like two boxers, they stared at each other, eyeball-to-eyeball.

Saint-Exupéry's close brush with death recalls the words of John McLelland in his book *The Clown and the Crocodile:* "One day a group of people will go to a cemetery, hold a brief service, and return home. All except one; that will be you."

"It's too bad that dying is the last thing we do," says Robert Herhold, "because it could teach us so much about life."

The meditations that follow deal with death. The grace you ask for in each meditation is the following:

Lord, teach me about death,
that it may teach me about life.

During the week ahead—and during the rest of the weeks that follow—continue to do a nightly assessment of each day.

Spiritual directors also recommend that you occasionally assess your daily meditation exercise. This means that right after your prayer you take a moment to evaluate how well it went. If it went well, thank God. If not, try to find out why. For example, did you—

• prepare your mind and body properly?
• put yourself in God's presence?
• use your *imagination* (to experience the exercise), your *mind* (to ponder it), your *heart* (to express your feelings to God), and your *soul* (to listen to God speak to you)?

Finally, did you take the time to record any insights or helpful ideas or thoughts in your journal entry?

Day one

> *"Behold, I am coming like a thief."* Revelation 16:15

A merchant in ancient Baghdad sent his servant to the marketplace to buy supplies. Minutes later the servant returned, trembling from head to foot. He said:

Master! Master! As I walked through the market, I was jostled by someone in the crowd. When I looked to see who it was, I saw it was Death. He peered at me threateningly. Lend me your fastest horse that I may flee to far-off Samarra. He will never think of looking for me there.

The merchant obliged, and his servant galloped off. Meanwhile the merchant went to the marketplace to buy the rest of the supplies. Lo and behold, who should he see but Death. "Why did you give my servant such a threatening look this morning?" the merchant demanded. "That wasn't a threatening look," said Death. "It was a surprised look. I was amazed to see your servant in Baghdad, for I had an appointment with him tonight in far-off Samarra."

Do you look upon death as an end of life or as a beginning of a new life? *Speak to Jesus about how he viewed his own death.*

_____

_____

_____

_____

_____

_____

_____

_____

Day two

"My soul is sorrowful even to death."   Matthew 26:38

Al Dewlen wrote an article about his son Mike, who was killed in Vietnam.

Al got the news one Friday evening. He had just returned from the office and was standing over a messy workbench in his garage, trying to decide what job to tackle before supper.

Suddenly he heard his name. He looked up and saw his wife and the pastor of his church standing in the doorway. Al's jaw dropped. "What's wrong?" he asked. "Mike's been killed," his wife replied.

Immediately Al lost all contact with reality. His mind flashed back across the years. First, he saw Mike as a six-year-old, playing Little League baseball. Next, he saw Mike as captain of the high school's football team. Finally, he saw him in his Marine uniform. Mike was a son he was truly proud of.

Al said later that the news left him so shocked that he was unable to speak to his wife or take her in his arms. All he could think of was Mike, lying cold, lifeless, and still.

Imagine your family getting the news of your death. *Picture Jesus greeting you after your death.*

Day three

It is appointed that human beings die once.

All the world's a stage,
And all the men and women merely players:
They have their exits and their entrances;
And one man in his time plays many parts,
His acts being seven ages. At first the infant,
Mewling and puking in the nurse's arms. . . .
Then the whining school-boy, with his satchel
And shining morning face, creeping like snail
Unwillingly to school. And then the lover,
Sighing like furnace, with a woeful ballad. . . .
Then a soldier,
Full of strange oaths . . .
Seeking the bubble reputation. . . .
And then the justice . . .
With eyes severe and beard of formal cut. . . .
The sixth age shifts
Into the lean and slipper'd pantaloon . . .
and his big manly voice,
Turning again toward childish treble, pipes
And whistles in his sound. Last scene of all,
That ends this strange eventful history,
Is second childishness, and mere oblivion,
Sans teeth, sans eyes, sans tastes,
sans everything.   William Shakespeare, *As You Like It*

What stage of life are you in? How does the last stage help to clarify the purpose of life? *Speak to Jesus about this.*

_____

_____

_____

_____

Day four

*"What eye has not seen,
and ear has not heard,
and what has not entered the human heart,
what God has prepared
for those who love him,"
this God has revealed to us
through the Spirit.*   1 Corinthians 2:9–10

Colonel David Marcus was killed in the Israeli War in June 1948. In his wallet was a card about death. It read:

I am standing upon the seashore. A ship at my side spreads her white sails to the morning breeze and starts for the ocean. She is an object of beauty and strength. And I stand and watch her, until at length she is only a ribbon of white cloud just where the sea and sky come to mingle with each other. Then someone at my side says, "There! She's gone!" Gone where? Gone from my sight—that is all. She is just as large in mast and hull and spar as she was when she left my side, and just as able to bear her load of living freight—to the place of destination. Her diminished size is in me, not in her. And just at the moment when someone at my side says, "There! She's gone!" there are other voices ready to take up the glad shout, "There! She comes!" And that is dying.

How does this view of death agree with the Bible's view? *Speak to Jesus about life after death and how you should be preparing for it now.*

Day five

"Father,
into your hands I commend my spirit."
Luke 23:46

In his book *Through the Valley of the Kwai,*
Ernest Gordon describes the death of a young prisoner
of war. It was clear to those around him that he was
struggling with death. Then one of the prisoners
opened a tattered Bible and began to read to the boy:

The LORD is my shepherd; I shall not want. . . .
Even though I walk in the dark valley
I fear no evil;
for you are at my side.   Psalm 23:1, 4

The boy's eyes grew peaceful. Then he said
calmly, "Everything is going to be all right now." A
few seconds later, he died.

Consider another case. In her last interview
before her death, Ethel Waters, the famous gospel
singer, said, "I'm not afraid to die, honey. . . . I know
the Lord has his arms wrapped around this big, fat
sparrow."

Ethel Waters loved much. And if God is love, as
the Bible says, then there is nothing to fear—
especially for one whose heart was as big as her body.

Are people more afraid of dying than they are of
death? *Speak to Jesus about your greatest fear.*

_____

_____

_____

_____

_____

_____

Day six

The time is running out.   1 Corinthians 7:29

Buddy Holly skyrocketed to fame in the 1950s. The nineteen-year-old Texan was the first rock star to write, play, and sing his own music.

Holly's brilliant career spanned thirty-six months. During that time he wrote forty-five songs. Then a tragic plane crash ended it all. At the moment TV commentators flashed the news of his death to the world, six of Buddy's songs were on the best-seller charts.

If Buddy Holly could return from the grave and make one comment about life, he might quote Saint Paul's words to the Corinthians: "I tell you, brothers, the time is running out."

Why is death hard to accept, especially for a young person? Ernie Pyle, the immortal war correspondent, gave us a perceptive answer in one of his columns. He was describing a room filled with bomber pilots. They had just been assigned to a mission from which an average of one in four crews returned safely. What Pyle sensed most in that room filled with pilots was not fear. Rather, it was a deep reluctance to give up the future.

If death came for you tonight, what one thing about your future would you be most reluctant to give up? *Speak to God about why you treasure this one thing above all the others.*

_____

_____

_____

_____

_____

Day seven

"God said to him, 'You fool,
this night
your life will be demanded of you.' " Luke 12:20

Three student devils in hell were packing their bags. They were about to be beamed up to earth for some on-the-job experience.

When all was ready, they reported to their teacher for last-minute instructions. The teacher asked them what strategy they had decided to use to get people to sin.

The first devil said, "I think I'll use the tried-and-true approach. I'll tell people, 'There's no God, so sin up a storm and enjoy life.' " The teacher nodded approvingly. Then he turned to the second devil and said, "What about you?"

The second devil said, "I think I'll use a more up-to-date approach. I'll tell people, 'There's no hell, so sin up a storm and enjoy life.' " Again, the teacher nodded approvingly. Then he turned to the third devil and said, "What about you?"

The third devil said, "I think I'll use a more down-to-earth approach. I'll simply tell people, 'There's no hurry, so sin up a storm and enjoy life.' "

Which of these three approaches would tempt you most? *Speak to Jesus about why you would be most vulnerable to this approach.*

_____
_____
_____
_____
_____
_____

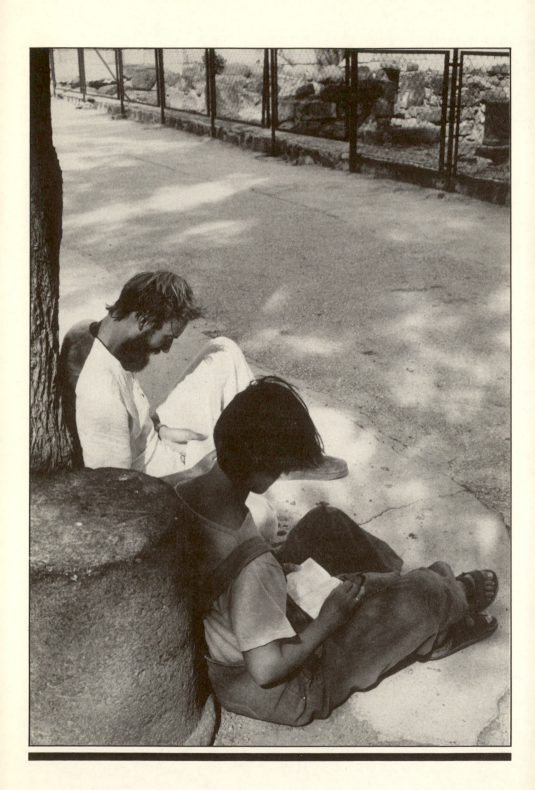

12
FORGIVENESS

Is your heart open to God's forgiveness?

If you, O LORD, mark iniquities,
LORD, who can stand?   Psalm 130:3

Someone kept holding up a sign during the 1984 play-offs between Detroit and Kansas City. It read, "Isaiah 55:7." Every time the television camera panned the first-base side of the infield, there was that sign.

A few days later two people recalled the incident. They got a Bible and checked Isaiah 55:7. It read:

Let the scoundrel forsake his way, and the wicked man his thoughts; let him turn to the LORD for mercy; to our God, who is generous in forgiving.

Isaiah's words remind us of something we tend to forget. You can no more undo a sin than you can "unring" a bell or "unfry" an egg. Sin can only be forgiven. And that's exactly what God does. He forgives us our sins, no matter how many or how great. Someone once said, "When we confess our sins, God casts them into the deepest ocean, gone forever.

Then God places a sign out there that says, NO FISHING!"

The meditations for the next seven days deal with God's forgiveness. They try to deepen our appreciation of God's incredible mercy. The grace you ask for in each meditation is this:

Lord, show me that there's a wideness
in your mercy
like the wideness in the sea.

Chapter 9 mentioned that the Holy Spirit might put into your heart a desire to celebrate the sacrament of Reconciliation. If that didn't happen then, perhaps it may this week. You may even feel moved to make a "general confession" of your entire life. Should this happen, ask a priest or your spiritual director how to do it.

Day one

How could I give you up?   Hosea 11:8

The prophet Hosea speaks of God's love and forgiveness in a moving and touching way. Speaking in God's name, he says:

When Israel was a child I loved him,
out of Egypt I called my son.
The more I called them,
the farther they went from me. . . .
Yet it was I who taught Ephraim to walk. . . .

How could I give you up, O Ephraim,
or deliver you up, O Israel? . . .
My heart is overwhelmed,
my pity is stirred.

I will not give vent to my blazing anger . . .
for I am God and not man,
the Holy One present among you;
I will not let the flames consume you . . .
says the LORD.   Hosea 11:1-3, 8-9, 11

Pray these words slowly, substituting your name where the name *Israel* occurs. *Pray the words again, only this time pray them in a whisper, imagining you are God speaking to himself.*

Can a mother forget her infant,
be without tenderness
for the child of her womb?
Even should she forget,
I will never forget you.   Isaiah 49:15

A woman dropped a beautiful orange vase on the kitchen floor; it splintered into dozens of tiny pieces. She swept the pieces up and threw them into the wastebasket.

An hour later she discovered her little daughter had retrieved the pieces from the wastebasket and had pasted them on a piece of white cardboard. Then, using a green crayon, the little girl had drawn stems and leaves on each piece, converting them into a beautiful bouquet of orange flowers.

The woman was moved to tears. Her daughter had seen something in the broken pieces that she had not seen. Where she had seen trash, her daughter had seen treasure. From what she considered to be something ugly, her daughter had fashioned something beautiful.

God does the same thing with people. God retrieves us from the wastebasket of sin and fashions us into something beautiful.

Do you really believe that God can take you after you have been broken by sin and fashion you into something even more beautiful than you are now? *Speak to God about this mystery of forgiveness.*

Day three

God . . . is rich in mercy. Ephesians 2:4

One of the strangest plays in Rose Bowl history occurred on New Year's Day, 1929. Roy Riegels of the University of California picked up a Georgia Tech fumble and ran it back sixty-five yards in the wrong direction. His own players eventually tackled him.

When California attempted to punt, Tech blocked the kick and scored a safety, which was Tech's ultimate margin of victory.

At halftime, Riegels expected the worst from Coach Price. But Price didn't mention the wrong-way run. When halftime was over, the California coach put his hand on Roy's shoulder and said, "The game's only half over. Give it your all!" Roy did.

This story makes a point that we find woven into the fabric of the Gospels. The God of Jesus is a God of the second chance. Yea, even more! The God of Jesus is a God of the third, fourth, fifth, and infinite chance. The God of Jesus forgives not seven times, but seventy times seven. The God of Jesus is rich in mercy.

Why do you think God is willing to forgive you so many times? *Speak to God about your willingness to forgive others as he has forgiven you.*

_____

_____

_____

_____

_____

_____

_____

_____

125

Day four

*Cleanse me of sin . . .
that I may be purified.*   Psalm 51:9

A newspaper columnist wrote about a program for removing tattoos—especially gang-related ones—from the bodies of young people. A surprising thing then happened. Thousands of letters came in from people all over the country for more information on the program.

Because of the remarkable response, the Los Angeles School District and a local cable television company produced a film called *Untattoo You*. It told about the dangers of amateur tattooing and showed how difficult it is to remove small tattoos from arms and faces and larger ones from chests and backs.

The stars of the film were the young people themselves. They talked frankly about why they were tattooed in the first place and why they now wanted the tattoos removed.

This story makes an important point. All of us have done things in our lives that we now regret and would like to erase. Thanks to the mercy of God, this is possible. All it takes on our part is a desire to be forgiven and an admission of our guilt.

Do you ever feel that you are not deserving of God's forgiveness? Why? *Speak to God about these feelings.*

Day five

You have been freed from sin. Romans 6:22

A soldier in Indonesia bought a monkey for a pet. Soon he noticed that the monkey was sensitive around the waist. Taking a look, he found a raised welt around the monkey's midsection. Pulling back the hair from the welt, he saw the problem.

When the monkey was a baby, someone tied wire around its middle and never took it off. As the monkey grew larger, the wire embedded itself into the monkey's flesh.

That evening the soldier began the task of removing the wire. Using a safety razor, he shaved the hair around the wire. Then he carefully removed it.

All the while, the monkey lay there with amazing patience, blinking its eyes. As soon as the operation was over, the monkey jumped up and down, leaped on the soldier, and hugged him tightly.

At one time or another in our lives, God has freed us from some sin that held us bound and in pain. The pain of confessing that sin was nothing compared to the pain of being held bound by it.

What makes you most reluctant to confess your sins? *Speak to God about the value of confessing your sins and admitting your wrongdoing.*

_____

_____

_____

_____

_____

_____

_____

Day six

As long as I would not speak,
my bones wasted away with my groaning. . . .
Then I acknowledged my sin to you,
my guilt I covered not. . . .
You took away the guilt of my sin.   Psalm 32:3, 5

Years ago *This Week* magazine carried a moving story about a seventeen-year-old Dutch boy. He was a prisoner who had escaped from a Nazi camp during World War II. He was caught and sentenced to death. Shortly afterward, he wrote to his father:

The military court has pronounced a very heavy sentence upon us. Read this letter alone, and then tell Mother carefully. . . . In a little while at five o'clock it is going to happen . . . one moment, and then I shall be with God. . . . Is that, after all, such a dreadful transition? . . . I feel so strongly my nearness to God. I am fully prepared to die. . . . I think it is much worse for you than for me, because I know that I have confessed all my sins . . . and have become very quiet. [Signed] Klees

Blessed is the person who will be able to say at the moment of death what that boy said.

If you died right now, could you say what Klees said? *Speak to God about your readiness to appear before him in judgment.*

_____

_____

_____

_____

_____

_____

Day seven

*You took off my sackcloth
and clothed me with gladness.*   Psalm 30:12

British violinist Peter Cropper was invited to
Finland for a special concert. As a personal favor, the
Royal Academy of Music lent Peter their priceless
285-year-old Stradivarius violin. That violin was
known the world over for its incredible sound.

At the concert, a nightmare happened. Going on
stage, Peter tripped and fell. The violin broke into
several pieces. Peter flew home to England in a state
of shock.

A master craftsperson, Charles Beare, spent
endless hours piecing the violin together. Then came
the moment of truth. What would the violin sound
like? Peter's heart began to pound as he picked up the
bow and began to play. Those present couldn't believe
their ears. The violin's sound was better than before.

The story of that violin is the story of each one
of us. Sin nearly destroyed us, but the master
craftsperson, God, put us back together again. Our
"sound" is now more beautiful than it was before.

How is it possible that our sound can be more
beautiful after we have sinned and confessed it than
before? *Speak to God about the mysterious power of his
healing love.*

13
GRATITUDE

How grateful is your heart?

"Ten were cleansed, were they not?
Where are the other nine?
Has none but this foreigner
returned to give thanks to God?"   Luke 17:17–18

Daddy Long Legs is the story of an orphan girl who receives gifts from an unknown person. She grows through childhood, young adulthood, and womanhood, blessed with opportunities provided by her secret benefactor. She tries to imagine what he is like, but she doesn't know if her idea of him is correct.

Then comes the great day. She discovers his identity and is able to thank him face-to-face for all he has done for her.

As you finish the story, you think to yourself, "How sad it would have been for the young lady to go through life without being able to meet her benefactor and thank him."

The story of *Daddy Long Legs* is a parable of God and each one of us. God gave us the gift of life and continues to shower us with gifts throughout life. Unfortunately, many of us go through life without having thanked God, except on rare occasions. We take these gifts for granted.

The meditations this week focus on gratitude and the role it should play in the life of every Christian. The grace you ask for in each meditation is beautifully expressed in these words by the seventeenth-century poet George Herbert:

O Thou who has given us so much,
mercifully grant us one thing more—
a grateful heart.

In the course of the week the Holy Spirit may put into your heart a desire to express your gratitude to God in some concrete way. Be alert to this possibility, and consider what you might do to express your gratitude.

Day one

Be filled with thanksgiving.   Colossians 2:7 (TEV)

The *Dallas Morning News* carried a photo showing prisoners on a work-release program, restoring an old house.

Several days later one of the prisoners wrote a letter to the editor saying that the last time he had his picture in the paper was several years ago, when he was sentenced. He wrote:

It was a real joy to see my picture in your paper doing something good. . . . When I entered prison 18 months ago, I was a lot like the house we just remodeled. . . . But God took charge of my life and has made me a new creation in Christ.

The prisoner was echoing Saint Paul, who said, "Whoever is in Christ is a new creation: the old things have passed away; behold, new things have come." *2 Corinthians 5:17*   When God blesses us like this, there is cause for thanksgiving. Thus Saint Paul says to the same Corinthians, "Thanks be to God for his indescribable gift!"   *2 Corinthians 9:15*

To what extent have you let God take charge of your life? How grateful are you to God for what he has done for you? *Speak to God about this.*

_____
_____
_____
_____
_____
_____
_____
_____

Sing to God
with thanksgiving in your hearts.
Colossians 3:16 (TEV)

The famous marathon runner Bill Rodgers was a conscientious objector to the war in Vietnam. Instead of serving in the military, he was assigned to alternative service in a home for retarded men. One of those men affected Bill's life profoundly. Bill says:

Whenever I saw Joe, he seemed to be wearing a big, welcome-to-my-world smile. When I glimpsed him at therapy sessions or workshops, he was participating wholeheartedly, eager to learn and grow as much as he could.

The smallest act of kindness toward Joe or the smallest object given to him made him brim with gratitude. Joe found reasons to be grateful even in the most trying or difficult circumstances.

This impressed Bill. He admired Joe's ability to focus on the good things in life, no matter how small, and to overlook the bad things, no matter how big.

How able are you to focus on the good things of life and overlook the bad things? *Speak to God about how you can develop a more positive outlook on life.*

_____
_____
_____
_____
_____
_____
_____
_____

Day three

In all circumstances give thanks.
1 Thessalonians 5:18

Corrie ten Boom and her sister Betsie were put behind barbed wire during World War II for helping Dutch Jews.

One day they were moved to a shelter completely infested with fleas. "How can we live here?" Corrie cried out.

Then Betsie remembered a passage from the Bible that she had read that morning: "In all circumstances give thanks." So the two women gave thanks for their new shelter, fleas and all.

In the weeks ahead, they discovered a remarkable lack of supervision from the camp guards. They were able to talk freely—even read and discuss the Bible with other prisoners. One day Corrie discovered why.

Someone called through the prison door to ask the guards to come in and settle a dispute. They refused, saying, "Settle it yourselves. We're not entering that flea bag."

Now Corrie understood why their barracks was so loosely supervised. And her mind went back to the day when she and Betsie gave thanks for their shelter, fleas and all.

———

Can you recall a similar incident from your life? *Speak to God about how you profited from this experience and thank him for it.*

———————————
———————————
———————————
———————————

Day four

I will glorify him with thanksgiving.   Psalm 69:31

Mention Bugs Bunny and people smile. Mention Charlie Jones and people frown. But Bugs Bunny owes his popularity to Charlie Jones.

In the 1930s, Jones was a struggling artist in Warner Brothers Studio. He took over the Bugs Bunny project and developed it into one of Hollywood's best-loved cartoons.

At the same time, Walt Disney created the famous "Three Little Pigs" cartoon. Jones wrote Disney a letter of congratulations. Disney was so grateful that he wrote a note of thanks back to Charlie.

Years later, Disney lay dying in a hospital. Charlie visited him. During the visit, Disney recalled the letter Jones had written him thirty years earlier. He thanked him again for being so thoughtful. "I treasure your letter," he told Jones. "You're the only animator who ever wrote to me."

"God has two dwellings," says Izaak Walton. "One is in heaven, and the other in a meek and thankful heart."

When was the last time you congratulated or thanked someone? *Speak to God about how doing these things enriches both others and yourself.*

_____

_____

_____

_____

_____

_____

Day five

"Lend expecting nothing back."   Luke 6:35

John Hughes drove a taxi in New York City for over thirty-five years. He could fill a book with his stories.

One day he found an emerald ring in his cab. He racked his brain, trying to remember to which fare it could have belonged. Suddenly he remembered helping a woman with a lot of bundles.

He drove back to the spot where the woman got out. It took him two days to find her. When he did, he returned the ring. She didn't give him a reward. She didn't even thank him.

John said later, "I still feel good about the incident; I know I did what was right."

It's hard to say what is more impressive about that story: the woman's ingratitude toward John, or John's upbeat attitude in the face of the woman's callousness.

Blow, blow, thou winter wind!
Thou are not so unkind as man's ingratitude.
William Shakespeare, *As You Like It*

Have you ever had a similar experience? *Speak to God about your failure to show gratitude toward him in a concrete way.*

_____
_____
_____
_____
_____
_____
_____
_____

Day six

*Give thanks always and for everything
in the name of our Lord Jesus Christ
to God the Father.*   Ephesians 5:20

Henry Ward Beecher once made this revealing comparison.

Suppose someone gave you a dish of sand mixed with fine iron filings. You look for the filings with your eyes; you comb for them with your fingers. But you can't find them.

Then you take a tiny magnet and draw it through the sand in the dish. Suddenly the magnet is covered with iron filings.

The ungrateful person is like our fingers combing the sand. Such a person finds nothing in life to be thankful for.

The grateful person, on the other hand, is like the magnet sweeping through the sand. That person finds hundreds of things to be grateful for.

*For the flowers that bloom about our feet;
For tender grass so fresh and sweet;
For song of bird and hum of bee;
For all things we hear and see,
Father in heaven, we thank thee.*
                    Ralph Waldo Emerson

Replay your last twenty-four hours. Pick out one thing from that period that you are grateful for. *Express your thanks to God for it.*

_____

_____

_____

_____

_____

Day seven

I will give thanks to you, O LORD,
with all my heart. Psalm 138:1

A man risked his life by diving into a raging river
to save a boy. After the boy recovered, he said to the
man, "Thank you for saving my life." The man put
his arm around the boy and said, "That's okay, son!
Just make sure your life was worth saving."

What that man said to the boy, Jesus Christ
could say to each of us. "The greatest gift you can
give me for saving you is to make the rest of your life
worth saving."

This meditation ends the first phase of *The
Spiritual Exercises of St. Ignatius,* which focuses on
the "challenge" of living out the "Christian ideal."
These exercises are presented in such a way that the
meditator can stop at this phase or go on.

The second phase focuses on Jesus and how he,
personally, lived that ideal. In the words of the
Broadway musical *Godspell,* the second phase invites
you to get to know Jesus more "clearly" so that you
may love him more "dearly" and follow him more
"nearly."

Do you feel God is calling you to stop at this first
phase? Or are you being called to go on to the second
phase? Or is God, perhaps, inviting you to a third
option: to take a few months off to decide. *Speak to
God about his "personal will" for you.*

_____

_____

_____

_____

_____

APPENDIX A

Implementing
The Challenge Program

Challenge was piloted in two completely different settings: with students at Jesuit High School in Dallas, Texas, and with adults at Saint Elizabeth Seton parish in Plano, Texas.

First, the Jesuit High setting. A month before school started, Father Patrick Koch mailed this letter to fifteen students:

I hope the summer is proving pleasant and profitable for you. . . . This letter is an invitation— meaning that I'm going to make an offer which you may either accept or decline.

During the coming school year I would like to use a program of spiritual retreat and renewal with some selected juniors. For those who take part it will require at least ten minutes of meditation daily, and it would also involve meeting together once a week after school for about a half hour.

The meditation book we will be using is called *Challenge*. It is the first book of a three-book program. The chief qualities required of those taking part in this program would be faithfulness to the daily meditation and eagerness to improve their inner spiritual life. I would expect the students involved in this program would actually become a leaven in the school community.

The first meeting would take place at 3:30 p.m. on Friday, book sales day, in my office. If you would like to be a part of this small group, please give me a phone call within the next two weeks. If you do not feel inclined at this time, there may well be another opportunity next year. I just wanted you to know that your name was suggested to me by someone who thinks very highly of you, as I also do.

Ten of the fifteen students accepted. This was double the number Father Koch anticipated. He then sent a letter of confirmation to the ten students, stressing the twofold commitment of daily meditation and a weekly meeting.

———————————

The second setting was with adults at Saint Elizabeth Seton parish in Plano, Texas. The author put the following invitation in the parish bulletin:

Father Link is interested in organizing a prayer group (ten people) for a six-week meditation program based on *The Spiritual Exercises of St. Ignatius*. It will require two commitments: (1) ten minutes of daily meditation, and (2) attendance at weekly "sharing sessions." For further details contact Maggie Herrod before September 7 at the Religious Education Office.

Twenty people responded. The first five women and the first five men were chosen.

Although the meditations in *Challenge* take thirteen weeks to complete, the author and the DRE for adult education agreed that asking for a thirteen-week commitment would eliminate too many adults. People could commit to six weeks, but not to thirteen. The author would recommend this approach to pastors and DREs.

An excellent time for implementing this approach would be Lent. The six-week Lenten season would be ideal for the "group" phase of the program, based on the first six weeks of meditations in *Challenge*. The seven-week Easter season, ending on Pentecost, would be perfect for the "personal" phase of the program, during which each person could continue on his or her own, using the meditations in weeks seven through thirteen.

An audiocassette presenting a detailed discussion of how to implement The Challenge Program is available through Tabor Publishing for $7.95 (see order information below).

In addition, the photograph on the cover of *Challenge* is available in a 12-inch by 18-inch poster with the caption, "The more you accomplish in your day, the more important it is to take the time to pray." This poster makes an ideal keepsake for each person participating in The Challenge Program. It will serve as a constant reminder of the individual's commitment to prayer.

The poster price is based on the quantity ordered (the minimum order is $10.00):

5–10	$2.00 each
11–49	$1.55 each
50 or more	$1.10 each

To order the audiocassette (#T2500) or copies of the poster (#22A14), call or write:

Tabor Publishing
P.O. Box 7000
Allen, Texas 75002
Toll Free: 800–527–4747
(In Texas: 800–442–4711)

Prepaid orders add $3.00 for shipping and handling. Texas and California residents add appropriate sales tax.

APPENDIX B

Spiritual guide

The ideal spiritual guide for someone using this book is a spiritual director schooled in *The Spiritual Exercises of St. Ignatius*. If such a person is not available, a priest, minister, nun, brother, or lay person may serve as the spiritual guide.

The guide's role is to help the person using this book come to grips with the meditation exercises. The real work is between the meditator and the Holy Spirit. The guide is a kind of spiritual midwife in this important process.

The guide's role is particularly important when it comes to young people: high school or college students. In such cases, the guide also serves as a *guarantor,* in George Herbert Meade's famous use of the word.

Guarantors are "significant others" who are farther along in life than the young people they guide and affirm. They are not father-mother substitutes. They are simply adults who respect young people and are, in turn, respected by them. Guarantors are credible people who have earned a right to be heard. They are persons whom young people trust and feel at ease with.

When it comes to spiritual guidance, a guarantor is the kind of person described in the Japanese *Zenrin:* "If you wish to know the road up the mountain, you must ask someone who goes back and forth on it."

In other words, a spiritual guide is someone who is praying on a daily basis—or is willing to begin such a practice. A guide is one who values meditation enough to want to share it with others. A guide understands that you cannot really teach another person to pray. You can only share how you pray. A guide never forgets the words of Saint Therese of Lisieux:

One must banish one's own tastes and personal ideas and guide the other along the special way Jesus indicates for them, rather than along one's own particular way.

Finally, a guide is one who supports and encourages the meditator. This means being able to discuss the meditator's personal and home life, for these are bound to impact the meditator's ability to pray and come to grips with the exercises.

It goes without saying, therefore, that a guide must be secure enough to be rejected by a meditator and resilient enough to weather the difficult situations that may arise. Insecure people should not guide other people. Success is too important to them. The best guides are often people who are successful in another job in life. This success gives them the security they need to let the Holy Spirit work in the Spirit's own time and own way.

A word about *The Spiritual Exercises of St. Ignatius.* Their goal is to help people find, choose, and live out God's will for them.

The Exercises are divided into four parts, called "Weeks":

First Week—invites you to evaluate how well you are living your life according to the purpose for which God created you.

Second Week—shows how Jesus lived his life according to the purpose for which his Father sent him into the world, and invites you to imitate and follow Jesus.

Third Week—strengthens and confirms your resolve to imitate and follow Jesus.

Fourth Week—launches you on your journey with Jesus to a fuller and richer Christian life.

This book, *Challenge,* treats the first week. The second book in this series, *Decision,* treats the second week. The third and final book in the series, *Journey,* treats the third and fourth weeks.

A popularized "text" of *The Spiritual Exercises of St. Ignatius* is *Modern Spiritual Exercises: A Contemporary Reading of the Spiritual Exercises of St. Ignatius* by David Fleming, available in Image (Doubleday) paperback.

APPENDIX C

Small group meetings

The ideal group size is about eight to ten members, who meet weekly after completing each chapter. Begin each weekly meeting with the following prayer:

*Lord Jesus, you said that
wherever two or three gather in your name,
you are there with them.
We are two or three;
we are gathered in your name;
and we believe you are with us.*

*May all our thoughts and sharing
be guided by the Spirit and directed solely
to the greater honor and glory
of God, our loving Father.*

End each meeting with a Scripture reading (see suggested readings below). Allow a few minutes of silence following the reading. As the group solidifies in trust, the silence may be followed by a brief shared prayer. Conclude each meeting by having everyone join hands and pray aloud the Lord's Prayer.

The *first meeting* is a get-acquainted session. If group members do not know each other, introductions are in order: name, birthday, birthplace, hobby, special interest, and so on. Next, members might describe their present prayer practice: when they pray, how often, how long, the form their prayer takes.

Next, members might explain why they decided to become involved in this meditation program and how they hope to benefit from it.

Finally, copies of *Challenge* may be distributed. Depending on the time available, members might take turns reading out loud and discussing the introductory section: "How to Use This Book."

A "sharing guide" for *subsequent meetings* follows. (One question is related to each meditation. Not all questions need to be taken. Nor do the questions have to be taken in the order shown.)

One final, important point. Each group session should routinely begin with three preliminary questions:

1. What time, place, and posture did you use for your daily meditation? (This question may be dropped after all group members have settled upon a definite time, place, and posture.)
2. Which daily meditation for this week did you find especially fruitful?
3. Would you mind sharing your journal entry for that meditation with the group?

WEEK 1 *Who are you?*
Scripture reading: Psalm 8

1. What are three significant answers you would give to the question "Who am I?"
2. What three words best describe you? Explain.
3. What is one thing you really like about yourself?
4. What is one special or unusual talent you have?
5. How are you using your special talent to serve God and others?
6. What is one significant fact about yourself that is a source of joy to you, but that few people know about?
7. Explain how the parable about the eagle has relevance for you.

147

WEEK 2 *Do you rejoice in who you are?*
Scripture reading: Galatians 6:1-10

1. What is one thing you find somewhat hard to accept about yourself or your family situation?
2. When you feel hurt or in need of support, what person do you usually turn to?
3. What is the biggest challenge you have faced so far in life?
4. What event or experience taught you firsthand that life can be hard and cruel at times?
5. What is an example of something that began as a cross in your life and turned out to be a blessing in disguise?
6. What was one of the earliest successes you had in your life? What impact did it have on your subsequent life, if any?
7. What is one thing in your life that you fail to see as having value or meaning?

WEEK 3 *How meaningful is your life?*
Scripture reading: Mark 8:31-38

1. What is your greatest motivation for trying to live your life in a Christian way?
2. If you could relive one day of your life, which day would it be and why?
3. On a scale of one (low) to ten (high), how happy are you? Explain.
4. What are three things you have thought about doing with your life? Explain.
5. Would you say you are currently following the high way, the low way, or the middle way? Explain.
6. Do you think you are a better Christian today than you were a year ago? Five years ago? How do you account for this?
7. Do you feel that you are sometimes "re-arranging deck chairs on a sinking ship"? Explain.

WEEK 4   *Who is God?*
Scripture reading: Psalm 104:24-35

1. Was there ever a time when you doubted God or your faith? How did you resolve your doubts? What questions do you still have about God or your faith?
2. What convinces you most that God is present and active in today's world?
3. Describe the most memorable experience you ever had with one or both of your parents.
4. Describe an experience you had that is similar to the one Bede Griffiths describes.
5. Do you agree with Kagawa when he says that Jesus dwells in a special way in the poor and needy? If so, why should Jesus do this?
6. Do you agree with Augustine when he says it is easier to say who God is *not* than who God *is?* If so, give an example to illustrate.
7. Why doesn't God show himself in modern times in more dramatic ways, as he did in biblical times?

WEEK 5   *How do you experience God?*
Scripture reading: Psalm 139:1-18

1. Which person of the Holy Trinity do you feel most comfortable praying to? Why this one?
2. Describe a time when you prayed to God with the same kind of urgency that King did.
3. What is one thing that keeps you from giving God a higher priority in your life?
4. Did you ever have an experience similar to the one Thor Heyerdahl had on the Oxtongue River?
5. Do you have a favorite prayer or poem that you carry in your wallet and pray on occasions?
6. In what sense does God live in you, or is this more or less a figure of speech?
7. Describe a serious illness that befell you and the effect it had on your relationship with God.

WEEK 6 *What is God's plan for you?*
Scripture reading: 1 Samuel 3:1-10

1. Why do you feel there has to be more to life than "money, TV, parties, and getting high"?
2. How realistic and reasonable is Sayers's "I Am Third" philosophy in our modern society?
3. Describe a time when somebody treated you with remarkable gentleness. Why is the phrase "gentle person" not as popular as it once was?
4. What is one flaw you have in your personality or character? How could God turn that flaw into an asset? Explain.
5. On a scale of one (low) to ten (high), how strong is your faith in God? Why do you find it hard to commit yourself to the spread of God's kingdom on earth with the same zeal that Luke displayed in committing himself to his mission?
6. What do you fear most about committing yourself more zealously to the spread of God's kingdom?
7. Explain your response to God's hypothetical question to you in this meditation.

WEEK 7 *What is your reaction to God's plan?*
Scripture reading: Genesis 22:1-12

1. What is one good thing you did this week that went almost totally unnoticed?
2. What is Amy's point in this meditation? How does it apply to you?
3. What is one thing you could do to greatly improve your chances of becoming the kind of person God wants you to be?
4. Are you more willing to sacrifice for temporal things than for eternal things? If so, how might you reverse this situation?
5. Using Dr. Judd's criteria, how ready are you to study medicine—or some other service-oriented career?

6. Can you accept Saint Ignatius' "First Principle and Foundation"? If not, how would you have to amend it to make it acceptable to you?

7. What is the point of the soldier's prayer? How does it apply to your life?

WEEK 8 *How aware are you of sin's power?*
Scripture reading: Romans 7:15-24

1. Which of your many gifts and talents from God are you tempted most often to use irresponsibly?

2. Someone once said, "Something isn't wrong because it's a sin; it's a sin because it's wrong." What did that person mean? Does the image of Christ being crucified for our sins ever enter your mind when you are being tempted? Why should it?

3. Why are so many people so violent today?

4. Why do you think another holocaust could or could not happen in twentieth-century America?

5. What are some collective sins being committed right now in your city? To what extent are you directly or indirectly involved in them?

6. What are some signs that suggest or indicate that what happened to the Ik is beginning to happen to Western society?

7. What is Golding's point, and how would you answer his question?

WEEK 9 *How aware are you of personal sin?*
Scripture reading: Psalm 51:1-13

1. Why are sins of omission, perhaps, more serious than sins of commission?

2. Describe an occasion when you made a personal sacrifice to help another, or when another made a personal sacrifice to help you.

3. How easily and readily do you admit that you are at fault, when this is the case? Do you feel that "honesty is always the best policy"?

4. What does it mean "to cheat" the man—or the woman—in the glass?
5. Describe some wrong you committed, and tell how you felt immediately after you did it.
6. Explain the difference between *knowing about* a person and *knowing* the person. Apply this to God.
7. How did you answer the question "What ought I to do for Christ in the future?"

WEEK 10 *How will God evaluate your life?*
Scripture reading: Matthew 25:31-46

1. What are some signs that the future holds good things for you? What are some signs to the contrary?
2. How is the parable of the building contractor a parable about your life?
3. What one sentence would you like to have inscribed on your tombstone?
4. What is the point of the Bandinelli story? How true is it, when applied to your own character?
5. Describe a religious or semireligious dream that you had. What kind of lasting effect did it have on your life?
6. Explain Camus's remark about judgment. How frightening do you find the thought of a final judgment?
7. Finish this sentence: "I would give anything to be . . ." Explain your response.

WEEK 11 *Are you ready to say yes to death?*
Scripture reading: Luke 12:13-20

1. What is the point of the Baghdad story? How frightened are you of death?
2. Which member of your family would take your death the hardest if you died tonight? Why that person?
3. Why do you think God allows the human body to deteriorate and become ugly with old age?

152

4. What is the point of Marcus's "poem" about death? If death is a "birthday" into a life of happiness with God, why do you want to postpone it as long as you can?
5. Would you prefer to die suddenly—in a car crash, perhaps—or after a brief, painless illness?
6. What three things in your future would you hate to give up most if you died tonight?
7. Which devil's approach would tempt you most? Least?

WEEK 12 *Is your heart open to God's forgiveness?*
Scripture reading: Luke 6:17-26

1. What effect did substituting your name and whispering this passage have on you?
2. Recall a time when God made something good out of something bad in your life.
3. What makes one person (Peter) trust in God's mercy, and another (Judas) despair of it?
4. Suppose your best friend said, "I know I'm going to go right on sinning, whether I confess my sins to God or not. Why should God forgive me, when God and I both know this?" How would you respond to your friend?
5. When did you last confess your sins to God?
6. If confessing to God brings such peace, why don't more people do it more often? Why don't you confess more often?
7. Why does God often pick unlikely people to do important jobs for him?

WEEK 13 *How grateful is your heart?*
Scripture reading: Luke 17:11-19

1. What is the biggest gift God has given you through this meditation program over the thirteen weeks you have been involved in it?

2. When was the last time you thanked someone, especially a family member, in an extra special way?

3. When was the last time you thanked God in an extra special way?

4. When was the last time you wrote a thank-you note to someone? Gave someone a thank-you gift?

5. How do you react when you go out of your way to help someone and that person is ungrateful, as the woman was in this story? Why do you think John was able to react the way he did?

6. What is one thing in the past twenty-four hours that you are truly grateful for?

7. What decision did you make concerning the next phase of the meditation program: to stop, to continue, or to think about it for a while? Explain your decision.